BREAKTHROUGH
FRENCH 2

SECOND EDITION

Stephanie Rybak

Brian Hill
General Editor
Head of the School of Modern Languages
University of Brighton

For Véronique and Chris

First edition 1998; Reprinted five times
Second edition 2003
Published by PALGRAVE MACMILLAN
Houndmills, Basingstoke, Hampshire RG21 6XS and
175 Fifth Avenue, New York, N.Y. 10010
Companies and representatives throughout the world

PALGRAVE MACMILLAN is the global academic imprint of the Palgrave Macmillan division of St. Martin's Press, LLC and of Palgrave Macmillan Ltd. Macmillan® is a registered trademark in the United States, United Kingdom and other countries. Palgrave is a registered trademark in the European Union and other countries.

ISBN 1-4039-1673-X book
ISBN 1-4039-1672-1 book and cassette pack
ISBN 1-4039-1674-8 cassettes

A catalogue record for this book is available from the British Library.

This book is printed on paper suitable for reycling and made from fully managed and sustained forest sources.

Designed by design@djhunter
Audio production for first edition: Anna Bentinck at John Green. Edited by Tim Woolf.
Additional audio production for second edition: Brian Hill. Actors: Philippe Monnet, Marianne Borgo, Jean-Pierre Blanchard, Nicolas Levoy, Thierry Chenevat, Magalie Charrier, Christine Diamond, Marc Gaudry

10	9	8	7	6	5	4	3	2	
12	11	10	09	08	07	06	05	04	03

Printed in China

Acknowledgements
The author is immensely grateful to: the many French people who took part in the Conversations on which the course is based; Christine Vaillant and Sophie Yékawéné, who organised the location recordings in Toulouse; those responsible for the editing and production of the course: Helen Bugler, Isobel Munday, Katie Lewis and Philip Tye; Muriel Campbell for native-speaker checks of the text.

The author and publishers wish to thank the following for permission to use copyright material: Brenda Nield for the photograph of Stephanie on p.3; Editions Jean-Claude Lattès for the extract from *La Jeune Fille au Pair* by Joseph Joffo on p.36, The New York Times Syndicate for the extract from an article in *L'Express* on p.39; ecolauto, Paris, for the extracts from their booklet *Codoroute* on pp.68 and 74; CNES for the photograph on p.86 and the third photograph on p.87; NASA for the first two photographs on p.87 and for the photograph on p.104; Hachette Livre for the extract 'Argent' from *Le guide du Routard: Réunion 97/98* on p.132; Maeva Loisirs for an extract from their brochure on p.138; *La Dépêche du Midi* for an article on p.154; Nicols for their letter on p.159; *la Croix* for an edited article on p.163; Anne Fontaine for the photograph on p.175. Other photographs by the author.

Every effort has been made to trace all copyright holders but if any have been inadvertently overlooked the publishers will be pleased to make the necessary arrangements at the first opportunity.

Contents

MAKING THE MOST OF THIS COURSE

Welcome to Breakthrough French 2

Breakthrough French 2 is intented for both self-study learners and classroom use. If you are using Breakthrough on your own, please do take the time to read through this introduction. You'll be able to get more out of the course if you understand how it has been structured and what is expected of you.

Breakthrough French 2 is designed to take you on from Breakthrough, or indeed any similar beginner's course. We have consulted hundreds of language learners on what they need at this level and the course has been built on their advice. Above all, people want a course which will enable them to cope in the real situation. Breakthrough French 2 combines authentic spoken French and authentic written French, so that you are prepared both for the informality of real speech and for the more formal style of the written language.

There are twelve units, each based on a theme which reinforces and extends your knowledge of real French. The emphasis is on the language used to understand and communicate effectively in a range of common situations. Each unit has the same basic structure.

1 The introductory page

This sets the scene, tells you what you will learn, reminds you of some key points from the previous unit and gives you a few tips on how to learn and what to watch out for.

2 Conversations

In each unit there are three Conversations in which the new vocabulary and structures are introduced. They have been specially recorded on location in France and cover different aspects of the unit theme. Please DO NOT expect to understand them immediately. By their nature, each one is introducing new vocabulary and structures. Try playing the Conversation through once or twice (reading the transcript at the same time if it helps). Then go through the Conversation using your PAUSE button and consulting the linked notes which explain things you may not yet have come across. Don't be afraid to make your own notes in the book or to underline things which are important to you. Finally, listen to the Conversation once or twice straight through without looking at the book before you move on to the practice section.

3 Practice

Each Conversation has a number of exercises attached to it. These pick up the main points from the Conversations and give you practice in reading, listening, speaking and, to a lesser extent, writing. Instructions on how to do each exercise are given in the book with answers, where appropriate, listed at the end of each unit. You will probably need to go through these exercises several times, particularly the speaking practice, before you feel you have mastered them. It's wise to spend as much time as you need here so that you really do learn the main words and structures.

4 Key words and phrases

To help you pull together the most important points, each unit has a Key words and phrases page which follows the Conversation and Practice sections. Read these through, checking back to the notes linked to the Conversations if you need to refresh your memory. Then work through the list, first covering up the French translation to see if you can remember the matching phrase in English, then covering up the English to see if you can remember the French.

5 Grammar

This is not a grammar course. The Conversations have been selected on the basis of the topic and the vocabulary they introduce. However, it is often valuable, and indeed interesting, to see how the language works. This can increase your confidence in generating language of your own. Each unit explains a few important aspects of grammar which should help you develop a firmer foundation. Interspersed are exercises to practise the points which have been introduced. If you can't get on with grammar, look at this section more for reference rather than feeling you need to have mastered everything before moving on.

6 Further practice

Each unit ends with one or two final activities. If you are able to work with a partner, there are suggestions on how to tackle them together. They have, however, been designed so that you can also work on them alone. The aim is to reinforce key points that have cropped up during the unit.

7 At the end

At the end of the book are a glossary of grammatical terms, verb tables, a list of the numbers, a vocabulary list and a grammar index.

A few final words

Be patient with yourself . . . above all don't get discouraged. Everybody comes across sticky patches when they feel they are not getting anywhere. Try looking back to some earlier Conversations to see just how much you have learned.

If you can, practise regularly. Thirty to forty minutes a day is usually better than a block of four hours once a week.

It helps to speak out loud in French as much as possible. This may seem strange at first but actually using the words, with a friend or to yourself, is a good way of practising and remembering.

There is a lot of material to take on board. Have confidence in us. Real language is quite complex and the course has been designed to build up your knowledge slowly, selecting what is important at each stage.

Bon courage!

Brian Hill

1 IT HAPPENED LIKE THIS...

WHAT YOU WILL LEARN
▶ understanding accounts of past events
▶ saying what has happened to you
▶ using the perfect tense
▶ something about New Caledonia
▶ car language

Le Capitole – the Town Hall in Toulouse

POINTS TO REMEMBER

You should read the introduction on p. iv: it will tell you what to expect from the course and how to get the most out of it.

If you haven't used authentic recordings before, you may find the Conversations a bit of a shock, because they are real French, spoken at normal speed by ordinary people, with all the hesitations and informality of natural speech. The course uses these authentic recordings to teach listening skills because they prepare you to understand the language in the real situation.

BEFORE YOU BEGIN

All the Conversations in this unit contain examples of the main past tense, known as the perfect or **passé composé**. It runs like this:

j'ai travaillé	**nous avons travaillé**
tu as travaillé	**vous avez travaillé**
il a travaillé	**ils ont travaillé**
elle a travaillé	**elles ont travaillé**

In other words, it follows exactly the same pattern as the English perfect tense, which is made up of part of the verb 'to have' and a form called the past participle: *I have worked, you have worked, he has worked*, etc. The difference is that the French perfect is also used to convey the meanings *I worked, you worked, he worked*, etc.

How the Conversations were recorded

Christine

Stephanie Rybak m'a contactée parce qu'elle souhaitait faire des enregistrements de français pour une méthode qu'elle allait, qu'elle allait faire. J'ai donc essayé de trouver un certain nombre de personnes d'âges différents, de sexes différents, de…qui font des métiers différents. Je suis très occupée et j'ai donc demandé à Sophie, qui est une jeune femme qui est extrêmement efficace, d'organiser tous ces rendez-vous – et c'est ainsi que ça s'est fait. Elle a réuni toutes ces personnes, elle a organisé l'emploi du temps; Stephanie est venue avec Anna, qui s'occupait des prises de son, et elles ont, pendant une semaine, rencontré une vingtaine de personnes qui ont discuté, donc, en français, de manière tout à fait naturelle.

LISTEN FOR...

Proper names:
- ▶ Stephanie Rybak (the course author, who asked Christine to find people to take part in the recordings)
- ▶ Sophie (who took over from Christine the task of organising the schedule)
- ▶ Anna (the audio producer, who went to Toulouse with Stephanie to make the recordings)

une méthode (here) a course
des enregistrements recordings

VOCABULARY

efficace	efficient
le métier	trade, profession
occupé(e)	busy
la vingtaine	about twenty
tout à fait	completely

Stephanie Rybak m'a contactée Stephanie Rybak [the course author] contacted me. For the extra 'e' on the end of **contactée**, see An optional extra … at the end of the Grammar section of this unit.

elle souhaitait she wished. This is from the imperfect tense of the verb **souhaiter**. This will be explained in Unit 3.

qu'elle allait faire which she was going to make. 'She is going to make a course' would be **Elle va faire une méthode**. 'She was going' is **elle allait**, from the imperfect tense.

j'ai donc essayé de trouver so I tried to find. The French equivalent of 'to try to do something' is literally 'to try of to do something': **essayer de faire quelque chose**.

j'ai donc demandé à Sophie […] d'organiser tous ces rendez-vous so I asked Sophie […] to organise all these appointments. To ask someone to do something in French comes out as 'to ask to someone of to do something': **demander à quelqu'un de faire quelque chose.**

c'est ainsi que ça s'est fait that's how it happened (literally, it is thus that that did itself).

Elle a réuni She gathered together. **Réunir** is 'to gather together', **se réunir** is 'to meet' (each other) and **une réunion** is 'a meeting'.

l'emploi (m.) **du temps** the schedule (literally, the use of time).

Stephanie est venue Stephanie came (literally Stephanie is come). There are a dozen so-called verbs of motion which form their perfect tense with the verb **être** rather than **avoir**. Unit 2 will review them.

qui s'occupait des prises de son who was in charge of the technical side of the sound recordings (literally, who occupied herself with the recordings of sound).

PRACTICE

1 On the basis of Conversation 1, identify the photograph of each of the speakers: Sophie, Stephanie, Christine or Anna.

J'ai écrit cette méthode

J'ai fait les prises de son

a

b

J'ai organisé l'emploi du temps

J'ai parlé dans la Conversation 1

c

d

a _____

b _____

c _____

Answers p. 16 d _____

2 Imagine that you have just organised a debate (**un débat**) for a radio station (**une station de radio**). On the recording,

- Jean-Pierre will ask you about it
- Philippe will tell you in English what you should say in French
- there will be a pause for you to stop your machine and speak
- Marianne will give a correct version of what you should have said

The verbs you will need are: **j'ai organisé**, **j'ai contacté**, **j'ai réuni** and **nous avons fait**. All your other words and phrases are in Conversation 1.

3 This letter is from the course author to Sophie, who set up the contacts and schedule for the authentic recordings of the course. You are not expected to understand every word in the letter, but read it through three times before tackling the questions below.

> *le 1er mars*

> **Chère Sophie,**
>
> **Voici enfin notre nouvelle méthode de français! J'espère que tu vas l'aimer! Je suis sûre, au moins, que tu vas être contente d'entendre tes amis sur les cassettes et de voir leurs photos dans le livre. J'ai utilisé ta voix plusieurs fois dans la méthode. As-tu vu ta photo? Anna et moi, nous te remercions de nouveau de tout le travail que tu as fait pour nous: tu as été d'une efficacité vraiment remarquable. Les participants que tu nous as trouvés ont été excellents – et très, très gentils en même temps – et l'emploi du temps a été parfait. Pour tout, bravo – et un très, très grand merci!**
>
> **Amitiés,**
>
> **Stephanie**

a See if you can find in the letter the French words for

at last _____

pleased _____

the book _____

your voice _____

several times _____

efficiency _____

at the same time _____

b If Stephanie had still been on '**vous**' terms with Sophie, how would the letter have looked? Fill in the gaps with **vous**, **votre**, **vos**, **avez** or **allez** as appropriate.

Voici enfin notre nouvelle méthode de français! J'espère que _____ _____ l'aimer! Je suis sûre, au moins, que _____ _____ être contente d'entendre _____ amis sur les cassettes et de voir leurs photos dans le livre. J'ai utilisé _____ voix plusieurs fois dans la méthode. _____ – _____ vu _____ photo? Anna et moi, nous _____ remercions de nouveau de tout le travail que _____ _____ fait pour nous: _____ _____ été d'une efficacité vraiment remarquable. Les participants que _____ nous _____ trouvés ont été excellents – et très, très gentils en même temps – et l'emploi du temps a été parfait. Pour tout, bravo – et un très, très grand merci!

| Answers p. 16 |

Unit 1 It happened like this...

New Caledonia

Séverine	Alors, Sophie – de quelle origine es-tu?
Sophie	Eh bien, ma mère, elle est de la Vendée, et mon père de la Nouvelle-Calédonie.
Séverine	Et tu es déjà allée là-bas?
Sophie	Oui, j'y ai vécu trois ans…et j'ai visité tout le pays.
Séverine	Et alors, qu'est-ce que tu as vu de beau?

Sophie Ben…un pays à la végétation très variée, une végétation très luxuriante…alors, par exemple, à Grande Terre, c'est très montagneux, et, pour faire le tour de l'île, il faut, il faut une jeep, une jeep, parce que les routes ne sont pas toujours goudronnées. Ce que j'ai remarqué là-bas aussi, c'est que la mer est bleue, bleue, transparente, et tu n'as personne sur les plages.

Séverine Et il y a des requins?

Sophie Oui, il y a des requins! Et il y a pas que des requins: il y a aussi des serpents de mer. Le danger en Nouvelle-Calédonie est plus dans l'eau que sur la terre.

LISTEN FOR...

j'y ai vécu	I lived there
montagneux	mountainous
tu n'as personne	you have nobody
des requins	sharks

Proper names:

la Vendée	a **département** of France
la Nouvelle-Calédonie	New Caledonia
Grande Terre	the principal island

VOCABULARY

le pays	country
luxuriant(e)	lush
par exemple	for example
le tour de l'île	the tour of the island
une jeep	a jeep
la route	road
toujours	(*here*) always (*also* still)
goudronné(e)	asphalted
le serpent de mer	sea-serpent

de quelle origine es-tu? where do you come from? (literally of what origin are you?)

ma mère, elle est de la Vendée my mother, (she) is from la Vendée (a **département** on the Atlantic coast of France).

et mon père, de la Nouvelle-Calédonie and my father from New Caledonia (a French overseas territory east of Australia in the South Pacific).

Grande Terre the island of New Caledonia itself, as opposed to the other islands which are dependencies of it.

tu es déjà allée là-bas? have you already been there? **Aller** is one of the 'verbs of motion' which form their perfect with the verb **être** instead of **avoir** (here, **es** rather than **as**). Unit 2 will focus on them.

j'y ai vécu trois ans I lived there for three years. **J'ai vécu** is from the perfect tense of the verb **vivre**. **Y** means 'there' – it always goes before the verb, as in **il y a**, 'there is' 'there are'.

qu'est-ce que tu as vu de beau? what beautiful things did you see? (what did you see of beautiful?)

un pays à la végétation très variée a country with very varied vegetation. **A** is often used when giving the attributes of something: **une glace à la vanille** 'a vanilla ice-cream'; **un pull à manches longues** 'a long-sleeved sweater'.

il faut une jeep you need a jeep. Sophie corrects her own pronunciation of **une jeep**. You can use **il faut** 'it is necessary' with a noun, as here, or with an infinitive: **Il faut conduire à droite** 'You have to drive on the right.'

ce que j'ai remarqué...c'est que... what I noticed... is that... (literally that which I noticed...it is that...).

tu n'as personne sur les plages you have nobody on the beaches. **Ne** and **personne** together make 'nobody'.

il y a des requins? are there any sharks?

il [n'] y a pas que des requins there aren't only sharks. **Pas** is 'not' and **que** is 'only'. In written French, there would be an **n'** with them.

Le danger...est plus dans l'eau que sur la terre The danger...is more in the water than on land.

PRACTICE

4 You will need to reuse phrases from Conversation 2 to answer Marianne's questions about New Caledonia. Imagine that you know it well – and follow Philippe's lead. Jean-Pierre will give correct versions of your part after you have had a chance to pause your machine and speak.

5 If you relish the idea of a close encounter with a shark or a sea-serpent, a diving holiday in New Caledonia might be for you. Here's some more information, just in case!

LA PLONGÉE EN NOUVELLE-CALÉDONIE

▼ ▼ ▼

UN DES PLUS GRANDS ET DES PLUS ANCIENS RÉCIFS CORALLIENS DU MONDE, 1 200 KM, LE PLUS RICHE EN SPÉCIMENS DONT CERTAINS SPÉCIFIQUES A LA NOUVELLE-CALÉDONIE. DES PLONGÉES AUSSI RICHES QUE VARIÉES, PROPOSÉES SOUS FORME D'EXCURSION ET DE SAFARI.

OBLIGATOIRE: Certificat médical de non contre indication à la plongée et votre diplôme de plongée.

VOTRE HOTEL:
LE MALABOU BEACH HOTEL
Situé sur une magnifique plage de sable blanc à l'extrême nord de la Grande Terre. 37 bungalows de grand confort pour 2 à 3 personnes, avec air conditionné, douche, mini-bar, télévision, magnétoscope et téléphone. Séjour en demi-pension.

a See if you can find in the text the French words for:

diving _____

coral reefs _____

as rich as [they are] varied _____

video _____

b How long is the New Caledonian coral reef? _____

c What colour is the sand on the beach around the hotel? _____

d In what part of the island is it situated? _____

e What amenities are there in each chalet? _____

_____

f Are the arrangements full-board or half-board?

_____

g What two documents must you produce to be allowed on this holiday?

Answers p. 16

_____

6 Jean-Pierre has been on that diving holiday. On the recording, he talks about it and mentions other islands (**îles**) which he has visited. Listen two or three times and then tackle the questions.

a Do Marianne and Jean-Pierre call each other **vous** or **tu**? _____

b Which islands does Jean-Pierre say he has visited?

Saint-Pierre-et-Miquelon _____ Reunion _____

Tahiti _____ Mayotte _____

Martinique _____ Guadeloupe _____

c Why does Jean-Pierre say he chose to go to New Caledonia?

_____

d What does Jean-Pierre say about:

i. the island? _____

ii. the sea? _____

iii. the beaches? _____

iv. the fish? _____

Answers p. 16

v. the coral reef? _____

A stolen car

Anne	Tu sais qu'on nous a volé la voiture?	
Pierre	C'est pas vrai!	
Anne	Si! Hier, juste devant la maison, dans un quartier calme, résidentiel…	
Pierre	Mais cela a eu lieu quand?	
Anne	Hier soir – dans la nuit.	
Pierre	Devant chez toi?	

LISTEN FOR…

on nous a volé la voiture	someone stole the car from us
des pneus neufs	new tyres
casser une vitre	to break a window
des pièces	parts

Anne Oui, oui. En plus, c'était une vieille voiture…Bon, il y avait des pneus neufs – on pense que c'est pour ça – mais…il n'y avait aucune raison qu'on nous la vole.

Pierre Et…il y avait des clés dessus?

Anne Mais non, non, non – on ne comprend pas…on sait pas.

Pierre Ils ont dû casser une vitre.

Anne Non, on n'a pas retrouvé de, de bris de verre…Alors, bon, on nous a téléphoné aujourd'hui: on l'a retrouvée – heureusement – donc, on va demander à un voisin qu'il nous la bricole un petit peu parce que, évidemment, il manque des pièces.

Pierre Ils ont volé beaucoup de pièces?

Anne Oh…non, c'est réparable…ça va.

---

on nous a volé la voiture someone stole our car from us (literally one to us has stolen the car). **On** can mean 'someone', 'people' or 'we', depending on context.

C'est pas vrai! They haven't! Literally, That's not true! The correct written form would be **Ce n'est pas vrai!**, but these authentic recordings show up again and again the tendency of spoken French to drop the **ne**.

Si! Yes [it is]! **Si** (meaning yes) is used only to contradict a negative: **Tu ne vas pas sortir ce soir? – Si!** 'Oh yes I am!'

juste devant la maison just in front of the house.

cela a eu lieu that took place. This is the perfect tense of **avoir lieu**, 'to take place' (literally, to have place): **Le spectacle a lieu à 21 h.** 'The show takes place at 9 p.m.'

c'était une vieille voiture it was an old car. **C'était** is from the imperfect tense of the verb **être**. The usual masculine form of **vieille** is **vieux**: **un vieux vélo** 'an old bicycle'.

on pense que c'est pour ça we think that's why.

il n'y avait aucune raison there was no reason. **Ne…aucun(e)** means 'no': **Je n'ai aucune idée** 'I have no idea'; **Elle ne fait aucun effort** 'She makes no effort.'

qu'on nous la vole to steal it from us (literally that one to us it steal).

il y avait des clés dessus? were there keys in it? **Dessus** is literally 'on top'. The opposite of **dessus** is the easily confusable **dessous** (underneath).

Ils ont dû casser une vitre They must have broken a window. **Dû** is the past participle of the verb **devoir** 'must': **J'ai dû laisser mes clés chez toi** 'I must have left my keys at your house.' **Une vitre** is used of a car window, but **une fenêtre** of a window in a house.

on n'a pas retrouvé de bris de verre we didn't find any broken glass. **Trouver** and **retrouver** both mean to find: the nuance of difference between them is very slight.

on va demander à un voisin qu'il nous la bricole un petit peu we're going to ask a neighbour to do a bit of work on it. **Bricoler** means 'to mend', 'to improvise' or to 'tinker with', **le bricolage** is 'DIY' and **un bricoleur** is someone who does it. These words can have negative connotations of botched jobs.

évidemment, il manque des pièces obviously, there are parts missing. **Il manque** is literally 'there lack(s)'. The French for 'I miss you' is **Tu me manques** or **Vous me manquez** – literally, You are lacking to me.

ça va it's OK. Also used in **Ça va? – Ça va** 'How are things? – Fine.'

PRACTICE

7 Here is part of a letter in which Anne tells a friend about the theft of her car. The words missing from the gaps are

retrouvé ont téléphoné volé pneus évidemment vieille maison

See if you can fill them in correctly.

Hier, nous avons eu un choc, parce qu'on nous a _____

la voiture juste devant la _____ . C'était notre

_____ Renault 4 – on ne comprend vraiment pas

pourquoi les voleurs _____ choisi cette voiture-là.

La seule raison possible, c'est qu'elle avait des _____

neufs. On nous a _____ de la gendarmerie cet

après-midi: on a _____ la voiture – sans pneus,

Answers p. 16

_____ .

In this advertisement for second-hand tyres, find the French for

a second-hand tyre _____

b guaranteed tyres _____

c open from Monday to Saturday _____

d free fitting _____

e all brands _____

f without appointment _____

g credit facilities _____

Answers p. 16 **h** at low prices _____

9

Des pièces... Here is some more vocabulary for car parts:
le pneu de rechange   spare tyre
la batterie   battery
l'ampoule (f.)   bulb
la boîte de vitesses   gear-box
le frein à main   hand-brake
la bougie (= candle)   spark plug
la courroie de ventilateur   fan belt
le parebrise   windscreen
l'essuie-glace (m.)   windscreen wiper
le bouchon de réservoir d'essence   petrol cap

First try to learn that vocabulary. Then listen to the recording, in which Jean-Pierre is buying various parts for his Renault 5, and put crosses by the Answers p. 16 four things he asks for.

10

Someone has stolen your hired bicycle (**le vélo de location**).
Working with the recording, you report it to the receptionist of your hotel.
All the words you will need to say have occurred in this unit
apart from the phrases: **on m'a volé un vélo / c'est très gentil / voici mon passeport**.

KEY WORDS
AND PHRASES

un enregistrement	recording
la méthode	course
j'ai essayé de trouver	I tried to find
des personnes	people
le métier	trade, profession
je suis très occupé(e)	I am very busy
j'ai demandé à Sophie	I asked Sophie
d'organiser	to organise
l'emploi (m.) du temps	the schedule
efficace	efficient
c'est ainsi que ça s'est fait	that's how it happened
tout à fait	completely
j'y ai vécu trois ans	I lived there for three years
j'ai visité tout le pays	I visited the whole country
qu'est-ce que tu as vu de beau?	what beautiful things did you see?
un pays à la végétation	a country with very varied
très variée	vegetation
pour faire le tour de l'île	to go round the island
il faut une jeep	you need a jeep
tu n'as personne sur les plages	you have nobody on the beaches
il y a des requins	there are sharks
on nous a volé la voiture	someone stole the car from us
devant la maison	in front of the house
dans un quartier calme	in a quiet area
cela a eu lieu (avoir lieu)	it took place (to take place)
des pneus neufs	new tyres
on pense que c'est pour ça	we think that's why
un petit peu	a little bit
il manque des pièces	there are parts missing

The past participles in the Grammar section are also key language for this unit.

GRAMMAR AND EXERCISES

The perfect tense

The perfect tense is used of actions which have been 'perfected', i.e. completed. Its basic pattern is given in Before you begin on p. 1. In the negative, the **ne** and **pas** go either side of the bit of **avoir**: **je n'ai pas travaillé, nous n'avons pas dansé**.

You need to learn the forms of past participles in order to avoid saying the equivalent of 'I have drinked' or 'I have readed'. However, when you make mistakes (as you inevitably will) people will generally understand you.

Learning past participles is made easier by the fact that most of them fall into groups:

Participles ending in -é

Working out the past participle of a verb which has an infinitive ending in **-er** is straightforward: it sounds exactly like the infinitive, but the ending is spelt **-é**, e.g. **essayé**, **parlé**, **commencé**.

Participles ending in -u

-u is the regular ending for the past participle of:

- verbs with infinitives ending in **-re**:

boire	to drink	**j'ai bu**
croire	to believe	**j'ai cru**
entendre	to hear	**j'ai entendu**
répondre	to answer	**j'ai répondu**
lire	to read	**j'ai lu**
perdre	to lose	**j'ai perdu**
vendre	to sell	**j'ai vendu**

- verbs with infinitives ending in **-oir**:

pouvoir	to be able	**j'ai pu**
savoir	to know	**j'ai su**
voir	to see	**j'ai vu**
vouloir	to want	**j'ai voulu**

- a few of the verbs with infinitives in **-ir**:

courir	to run	**j'ai couru**
tenir	to hold	**j'ai tenu**

Participles ending in -i, -is or -it

- With **-ir** verbs, the standard ending is **-i**:

dormir	to sleep	**j'ai dormi**
finir	to finish	**j'ai fini**

- Some verbs with infinitives in **-re** (including a number of irregular verbs) have participles ending in **-i**, **-is** or **-it** (which all sound the same):

suivre	to follow	**j'ai suivi**
mettre	to put	**j'ai mis**
prendre	to take	**j'ai pris**

(also **apprendre** and **comprendre**: **j'ai appris**; **j'ai compris**)

dire	to say	j'ai dit
écrire	to write	j'ai écrit
faire	to do, to make	j'ai fait (pronounced like the present tense il fait)

Participles ending in -ert

A few **-ir** verbs have past participles ending in **-ert**:

offrir	to give	j'ai offert
ouvrir	to open	j'ai ouvert
souffrir	to suffer	j'ai souffert

être and avoir

You would expect them to be irregular!

être	to be	j'ai été
avoir	to have	j'ai eu (one syllable, pronounced like the **u** in **tu**)

11 Write in each of the gaps the past participle of the verb given in brackets.
Une petite annonce = a small ad.

Nous avons [vendre] _____ notre vieille voiture la semaine dernière, alors nous

avons [vouloir] _____ en trouver une autre. Nous avons [lire]

_____ des centaines de petites annonces dans le journal et nous avons [finir]

_____ par en choisir quatre: des voitures d'occasion, toutes les quatre de

marque Peugeot. La première personne n'a pas [répondre] _____ au téléphone.

La deuxième m'a [dire] _____ que sa voiture était déjà vendue. La troisième a

[être] _____ tellement désagréable au téléphone que j'ai [refuser]

_____ d'y aller. J'ai donc [téléphoner] _____ à la quatrième

personne, une vieille dame charmante. Nous avons [courir] _____ chez elle et,

quand j'ai [voir] _____ son auto, j'ai tout de suite [savoir] _____

que c'était la voiture pour nous. Nous avons [faire] _____ un petit tour pour être

sûrs que la voiture roulait bien; j'ai donc [entendre] _____ le moteur – et c'était

comme un moteur neuf. C'est ainsi que nous avons [acheter] _____ notre

nouvelle voiture.

Answers p. 16

12 Translate into French:

a He has suffered. _____

b We have read the book. _____

c I have sold my house. _____

d They said hello. **Ils** _____

e I heard voices. _____

f You saw the photo. **Tu** _____

g You have lost the keys. **Vous** _____

h I have made the bed. _____

Answers p. 16

13 Test yourself on the verb-forms in this Grammar section:

- First cover up the infinitives in the list on pp. 12–13 and see if you can say the infinitive which corresponds to each of the perfect tenses.
- Then cover up the perfect tenses and see if you can remember the perfect which corresponds to each of the infinitives.

14 Write some sentences of your own using the perfect tenses listed in this unit.

_____

_____

_____

_____

_____

_____

_____

_____

_____

An optional extra for the grammatically minded...

You will sometimes see an extra **-e**, **-s** or **-es** on the end of a past participle. Compare
Stephanie a contacté Christine and **Stephanie m'a contactée** (where **m'** refers to a woman).
- Both **Christine** and **m(e)** are the direct objects of the verb. (Whom did Stephanie contact? Answer: **Christine/me**.)
- The past participle changes its ending to 'agree' with a feminine or plural direct object only if that object precedes the verb in the sentence.

  As-tu vu mes photos?   Have you seen my photos?
  Non, je ne les ai pas vues.   No, I haven't seen them.

It is not a priority for you to learn this rule.

AND FINALLY...

15 In this recording, Marianne plays the little old lady who was selling her car in Exercise 13. Your task is to make the initial phone call to her. Philippe will tell you what to say and Jean-Pierre will back you up after you have had a chance to speak. Your part includes the questions

- **Elle a quel âge?**
- **Elle a fait combien de kilomètres?**
  (**elle**, in both cases, being the car, not the old lady!) and
- **Est-ce que je peux venir voir la voiture?**

If you are learning with a partner, you can go on to roleplay a similar telephone conversation together.

16 Try answering the questionnaire. If you are working with someone else

- Partner A should close the book and reply to the questions.
- Partner B should ask the questions and write down the answers.

QUESTIONNAIRE

a   Quand avez-vous commencé à apprendre le français?

_____

b   Quels moyens avez-vous utilisés? (Livres, cassettes, radio, télévision, cours du soir...)

_____

c   Avez-vous beaucoup voyagé en France?

Oui ☐   Pas mal ☐   Non ☐

d   Avez-vous beaucoup parlé français avec des Français?

Oui ☐   Pas mal ☐   Non ☐

e   Dans quels contextes avez-vous eu l'occasion de parler français?

_____

_____

f   Pourquoi avez-vous décidé de faire du français maintenant?
    (Pour votre travail, pour votre plaisir, pour le parler en vacances...)

_____

g   Avez-vous bien suivi la première unité de cette méthode?

Oui ☐   Pas mal ☐   Non ☐

h   L' avez-vous aimée?
    Oui, beaucoup / Oui, assez / Non, pas tellement / Non, pas du tout

---

EXERCISE 1

(a) Stephanie   (b) Anna   (c) Christine
(d) Sophie

EXERCISE 3

(a) enfin / contente / le livre / ta voix / plusieurs fois / efficacité / en même temps   (b) vous allez / vous allez / vos / votre / Avez-vous / votre / vous / vous avez / vous avez / vous / avez

EXERCISE 5

(a) la plongée / récifs coralliens / aussi riches que variées / magnétoscope   (b) 1,200 km   (c) white
(d) the extreme north   (e) air conditioning, shower, mini-bar, television, video and telephone
(f) half-board   (g) a medical certificate saying there is no reason why you should not go diving and your diving certificate

EXERCISE 6

(a) tu   (b) Reunion, Martinique, Guadeloupe
(c) He loves islands   (d) i. It is beautiful and tropical. ii. You have never seen it so blue.   iii. There is nobody on them.   iv. They are exotic.   v. It is magnificent.

EXERCISE 7

volé / maison / vieille / ont / pneus / téléphoné / retrouvé / évidemment

EXERCISE 8

(a) pneu d'occasion   (b) pneus garantis
(c) ouvert du lundi au samedi   (d) montage gratuit
(e) toutes marques   (f) sans rendez-vous
(g) facilités de paiement   (h) à petits prix

EXERCISE 9

la batterie / la courroie de ventilateur / l'essuie-glace / le bouchon de réservoir d'essence

EXERCISE 11

vendu / voulu / lu / fini / répondu / dit / été / refusé / téléphoné / couru / vu / su / fait / entendu / acheté

EXERCISE 12

(a) Il a souffert.   (b) Nous avons lu le livre.
(c) J'ai vendu ma maison.   (d) Ils ont dit bonjour.
(e) J'ai entendu des voix.   (f) Tu as vu la photo.
(g) Vous avez perdu les clés.   (h) J'ai fait le lit.

2 TRAVEL

WHAT YOU WILL LEARN

- ▶ understanding accounts of journeys
- ▶ talking about your own travels
- ▶ understanding and giving accounts of accidents
- ▶ parts of the body
- ▶ using the perfect tense with **être**
- ▶ some names of countries

POINTS TO REMEMBER

In Unit 1 you learned to form the perfect tense with a part of **avoir** and a past participle on the model:

j'ai travaillé	nous avons travaillé
tu as travaillé	vous avez travaillé
il a travaillé	ils ont travaillé
elle a travaillé	elles ont travaillé

BEFORE YOU BEGIN

In Unit 2 you'll encounter the so-called verbs of motion, which form their perfect tense with **être** instead of **avoir**. So, for example, the perfect tense of **aller** goes like this:

je suis allé(e)	nous sommes allé(e)s
tu es allé(e)	vous êtes allé(e)(s)
il est allé	ils sont allés
elle est allée	elles sont allées

With these verbs, the past participle behaves like an adjective, i.e. it has a masculine or feminine, singular or plural ending to match the subject of the verb.

Matthieu's summer: at home, in Galicia and in the Ardèche

Matthieu

Alors cet été, tout d'abord le mois de juillet, je suis resté à Toulouse pour, pour travailler. Puis…je suis parti au mois d'août avec mes parents en voiture en Galice, au-dessus du Portugal. Le monde occidental n'est pas,

n'est pas entré dans cette région…elle est pas moderne, elle est encore très archaïque et…très sauvage. Ensuite, après être allé en Galice, je suis revenu à Toulouse, et de Toulouse je suis parti en Ardèche, une région qui se trouve à peu près au-dessus de la Provence, au-dessus d'Avignon, qui est une région aussi magnifique, là où…et là où j'ai passé une dizaine de jours avec…dix copains à moi, dans une maison tout seuls, coupés du monde et là où on a fait de la musique, on a joué, on s'est baigné et …et on a passé un très, très bon moment.

VOCABULARY

tout d'abord	first of all
archaïque	archaic
sauvage	wild
à peu près	approximately
une dizaine	about ten
jouer	to play

cet été this summer. The word for 'this or that' is **ce** (masc.), **cet** (masc., before a vowel sound) or **cette** (fem.).

je suis resté à Toulouse pour…travailler I stayed in Toulouse in order to work. Oddly enough, **rester**, 'to stay' or 'remain', counts as a verb of motion and forms its perfect with the verb **être** rather than **avoir**: **je suis resté(e), tu es resté(e), il est resté**, etc.

je suis parti I went off. **Partir** is used rather than **aller** when the emphasis is on going <u>away</u>, particularly for going off on holiday.

au-dessus du Portugal above (i.e. north of) Portugal. Portugal is one of the very few European countries to be masculine (see also p. 30). The opposite of **au-dess<u>us</u> de** is **au-dess<u>ous</u> de** 'underneath'.

le monde occidental n'est pas…entré dans cette région western civilisation (literally the western world) has not entered that region. **Entrer** is another of the 'verbs of motion'. Note that in the negative, **ne** and **pas** go either side of the bit of **être**: **n'est pas**.

encore still. It can also mean 'again': **Je suis encore retourné en Espagne** 'I went back to Spain again' or 'yet' when it comes in a negative sentence: **Je ne suis pas encore allé en Espagne** 'I haven't been to Spain yet.'

après être allé en Galice after having gone (literally after to be gone) to Galicia. Another example of **après** + infinitive:

Après avoir garé la voiture, ils sont allés au restaurant. After having parked the car, they went to the restaurant.

je suis revenu I came back. **Venir** is one of the verbs of motion. **Revenir** is one of its compounds, so follows the same pattern in everything.

en Ardèche to the Ardèche, which, despite what Matthieu says, is not a **région** but a **département** in the **région** of Rhône-Alpes.

dix copains à moi ten friends of mine. **Des copains** can be either all male or a mixed group. If they are all female, the word is **copines**. **Copain** and **copine** are more colloquial words than **ami** and **amie**, but they mean the same.

tout seuls, coupés du monde all on our own, cut off from the world.

on s'est baigné we bathed. From the verb **se baigner** (literally to bathe oneself). All reflexive verbs form their perfect with **être**.

on a passé un très, très bon moment we had a very, very good time.

PRACTICE

1 Here is a holiday even more remote than those described by Matthieu: a fortnight in French Guiana in the Amazon rainforest.

CIRCUIT
AVENTURE

SAÜL OU L'AVENTURE EXTRAORDINAIRE EN AMAZONIE FRANÇAISE

2 SEMAINES

Le village de Saül est comme une île, au cœur de la Guyane Française, véritable océan végétal. Né de la ruée vers l'or du début du vingtième siècle, il reste uniquement relié à Cayenne par avion. Une centaine d'habitants...Une seule cabine téléphonique...C'est dans ce cadre exceptionnel que nous vous proposons de vivre quelques jours, isolé du monde moderne.

la ruée vers l'or the gold rush
le cadre surroundings (literally frame)

a To what is Saül compared?

_____

b What brought the village into being?

_____

c How do you travel between Saül and Cayenne?

_____

d How many people live in Saül?

Answers p. 32

_____

2 The writer of the letter below has been on that holiday in French Guiana:

> Nous avons passé des vacances de rêve en Guyane! Le premier jour, nous sommes arrivés à Cayenne. Le lendemain, nous sommes repartis: nous avons pris l'avion pour Saül, un petit village au milieu de la forêt, où il n'y a qu'une centaine d'habitants, qui sont tous venus nous voir. Puis, quelques jours plus tard, nous sommes allés vivre en forêt profonde avec des bivouacs itinérants – nous y sommes restés pendant plusieurs jours. Nous avons vu des perroquets, des toucans, des tortues et des singes – et un bébé singe est né pendant notre séjour. Nous sommes aussi sortis de nuit pour approcher les animaux nocturnes. Ensuite, nous sommes retournés à Saül et puis à Cayenne, et nous sommes rentrés en France mardi. Cela a été une aventure inoubliable!

a Find in the letter the French for:

we went

_____

we came home

_____

a baby monkey was born

_____

we arrived

_____

we returned

_____

we left again

_____

we stayed there

_____

we also went out

_____

who all came to see us

_____

b Marianne gives the answers to question (**a**) on the recording. Repeat them after her for pronunciation practice.

Answers p. 32

3 Imagining that you have had the same 'unforgettable adventure', answer the questions Marianne puts to you on the recording. You'll need to use the verbs you were practising in Question 2, but saying **je** rather than **nous** (e.g. **je suis arrivé(e)** rather than **nous sommes arrivés**).

CONVERSATION 2

Anne's trip to Prague

Pierre Alors Anne, comment s'est passé ton voyage à Prague?

Anne Oh, très, très bien. Très bien. Vraiment, c'est une ville magnifique…

Pierre Tu es partie quand?

Anne Je suis partie en septembre, pendant une semaine, et…donc à une période un petit peu moins touristique – c'est agréable.

Pierre Et tu es partie comment là-bas – en avion?

Anne Ah non, là, par contre, c'était un peu plus compliqué: je suis partie de Toulouse en train, jusqu'à Paris. Là, j'ai changé: j'ai pris un autre train pour Strasbourg. Je suis restée quelques heures là-bas, le temps que…un bus arrive pour nous amener jusqu'à Prague – donc, tu vois, c'est un petit peu compliqué – en fin de compte, on y est arrivé et…voilà. C'était très agréable là-bas.

Pierre Et qu'as-tu visité à Prague?

Anne Ben, on est surtout resté dans les quartiers touristiques, bien sûr: les vieux quartiers historiques de la ville, qui, de toute façon, sont très riches en monuments, donc on a eu vraiment le temps de, de tout visiter…

Pierre Et sur Prague même, tu es restée combien de temps?

Anne On est resté quatre/cinq jours – cinq jours, je crois.

VOCABULARY

comment	how
vraiment	really
en avion	by plane
par contre	on the other hand
autre	other
surtout	above all
le quartier	district
de toute façon	in any case

comment s'est passé ton voyage? how did your trip go? **Se passer**, 'to happen', is a reflexive verb so forms its perfect tense with **être**.

Tu es partie quand? When did you leave? The same question addressed to a man would be written **Tu es parti quand?** The past participle behaves like an adjective when it accompanies the verb **être**.

pendant une semaine for a week.

un peu plus compliqué a little more complicated. (**Un peu** and **un petit peu** mean much the same.)

j'ai changé: j'ai pris un autre train I changed: I took another train. Not all verbs indicating movement form their perfect with **être**: many of them follow the standard pattern with **avoir**.

le temps que…un bus arrive pour nous amener the time [necessary] for a bus to arrive to take us.

en fin de compte on y est arrivé in the end we arrived there.

qu'as-tu visité? what did you visit? **Que** (or, here **qu'**) means 'what' – just like the longer **qu'est-ce que**.

on a eu vraiment le temps de […] tout visiter we really had time to visit everything.

sur Prague même in Prague itself.

4 Here is an extract from a letter:

Je suis allé à Toulouse l'année dernière, au mois de juin. Ma collègue Catherine et moi, nous sommes partis de Londres-Heathrow et, deux heures plus tard, nous sommes arrivés à Toulouse-Blagnac. Mon ami Jean-Claude est venu nous chercher à l'aéroport. Nous sommes descendus dans un hôtel du centre-ville pendant les trois/quatre jours de notre congrès. Ensuite Catherine est rentrée en Angleterre et moi je suis monté passer vingt-quatre heures chez Jean-Claude, qui a une belle maison sur les hauteurs de la ville. En fin de compte, j'y suis resté, non pas vingt-quatre heures, mais trois jours. Nous ne sommes pas beaucoup sortis, mais nous avons beaucoup parlé de notre travail et c'est à ce moment-là que notre nouveau projet est né!

Meilleurs souvenirs,

Sandy

Note: **descendre** (literally to descend) is used of staying at a hotel

a Is Sandy a man or a woman? How do you know?

_____

b When did Sandy go to Toulouse? _____

c How long did the flight take? _____

d Who met Sandy and Catherine at the airport? _____

e Where did Sandy and Catherine stay during the congress?

_____

f How long did the congress last? _____

g What did Catherine do afterwards? _____

h What did Sandy do? _____

i How long did Sandy end up staying in the house on the hill?

_____

j What did Sandy and Jean-Claude do?

_____

Answers p. 32

k What was the result of it? _____

5 On the recording, Marianne asks Jean-Pierre about his recent trip to Russia. You will hear the proper names (**la**) **Russie**, **Moscou**, **Léningrad**, **Saint-Pétersbourg** and **le Musée de l'Ermitage**. When you have listened several times, see if you can circle the correct replies to the questions below:

St Petersburg (from the top of St Isaac's Cathedral)

a	Which town did Jean-Pierre visit?	Moscow / St Petersburg
b	How did he get there?	Train / Plane
c	What was opposite the monastery?	Jean-Pierre's hotel / The Hermitage
d	How does Jean-Pierre describe the metro?	Touristic / Magnificent
e	How many hours did Jean-Pierre stay in the Hermitage Museum on his first visit?	Five / Six
f	How soon did he go back to it?	That evening / Two days later
g	How long was Jean-Pierre's stay in Russia?	A week / A fortnight

Answers p. 32

6 Your turn to speak: Jean-Pierre will ask you what you did at Christmas (**à Noël**). You tell him you went off to Greece (**en Grèce**) where you spent a week in Athens (**à Athènes**) and then went to Crete (**en Crète**). If you look at Conversation 2 before you begin it will help you prepare how to say 'The historical monuments are magnificent' and 'Christmas is a period that is a little bit less touristy'.

Séverine's accident-prone sister

Sophie

Et ta sœur, comment va-t-elle?

Séverine

Eh bien, justement, elle s'est encore cassé quelque chose! Elle a, en fait elle a glissé dans sa salle de bains et elle s'est complètement retourné le pied et donc elle a encore porté un plâtre pendant quinze jours, avec des béquilles…et elle n'arrête pas de se faire mal, en fait.

Sophie

Tu dis 'encore'…Pourquoi?

Séverine

Parce que…une fois, on était parti au ski et…et le premier jour où on est arrivé dans l'appartement, eh bien…elle est allée skier avec une amie qui avait un meilleur niveau qu'elle et elle s'est complètement retourné la jambe avec les skis croisés et elle s'est fait, par contre, une entorse, jambe re-dans le plâtre et…pendant les quinze jours, donc elle a vraiment pas de chance.

LISTEN FOR...	
elle s'est encore cassé quelque chose!	she has broken something again! (another bone)
elle a glissé	she slipped
des béquilles	crutches
une entorse	a sprain

VOCABULARY

en fait	in fact
le plâtre	plaster
pourquoi	why
une fois	once

comment va-t-elle? how is she? The '**t**' between **va** and **elle** does not mean anything but is inserted as a buffer between the two vowels when verbs are inverted in questions. Learn also **Comment allez-vous?** and **Comment vas-tu?** 'How are you?'

justement precisely. ('It's funny you should ask, because…')

elle s'est encore cassé quelque chose! she has broken something again! (literally she to herself has again broken something). French tends to avoid possessives like **son**, **sa**, **ses** or **mon**, **ma**, **mes** when talking about parts of the body. You have to say, for instance, 'I broke the arm to myself': **Je me suis cassé le bras**. (And an additional note for the very grammatically minded: if you are puzzled because **cassé** does not have a feminine ending in the Conversation, it is because what is broken is not 'herself' but 'something'.)

elle s'est complètement retourné le pied she twisted her foot completely (semi-literally, she to herself completely twisted the foot).

elle a encore porté un plâtre pendant quinze jours she again wore a plaster cast for a fortnight. The French count the first and the last dates in a fortnight (say, the 1st to the 15th of the month) and call it fifteen days. Similarly, you often hear **huit jours** for a week.

elle n'arrête pas de se faire mal she keeps on (literally, she doesn't stop) hurting herself.

on était parti au ski we had gone skiing. This is from the pluperfect tense, which pushes the action further back in the past than the perfect (**on est parti**). You don't need to use this tense yourself yet.

le premier jour où on est arrivé dans l'appartement the first day when we arrived in the apartment.

elle est allée skier she went skiing (literally she went to ski).

un meilleur niveau qu'elle a better level than her.

avec les skis croisés with the skis crossed

elle s'est fait, par contre, une entorse she gave herself a sprain that time. **Par contre** points up a contrast – its usual translation 'on the other hand' would be a bit confusing in this context of sprained limbs!

jambe re-dans le plâtre leg back in plaster. **Re-dans** is very colloquial in style.

les quinze jours the two weeks (of the holiday).

elle a vraiment pas de chance she really is unlucky.

PRACTICE

7

- ☐ **la tête**
- ☐ **le cou**
- ☐ **l'épaule** (f.)
- ☐ **le bras**
- ☐ **le coude**
- ☐ **le poignet**
- ☐ **la main**
- ☐ **le doigt**
- ☐ **la côte**
- ☐ **la hanche**
- ☐ **la jambe**
- ☐ **la cheville**
- ☐ **le pied**
- ☐ **l'orteil** (m.)

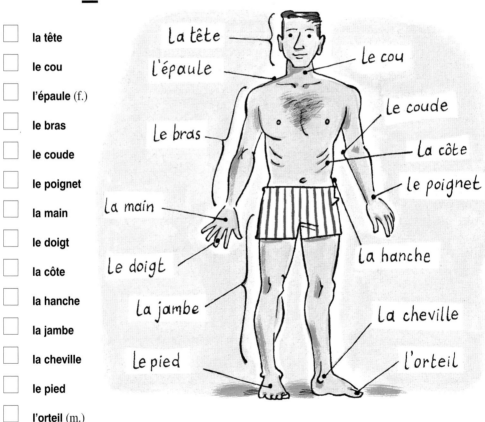

On the recording, Jean-Pierre talks about his passion for skiing – and the many bones he has broken because of it. Put a cross in the boxes corresponding to the ones he mentions.

Answers p. 32

8 Here is an extract from winter sports holiday brochure:

PYRÉNÉES

LES SPORTS D'HIVER SONT UNE FORMIDABLE OCCASION DE DÉCOUVRIR LES PYRÉNÉES DANS LEUR SIMPLICITÉ AIMABLE ET CHALEUREUSE.

225€

Prix minimum en 2 pièces 4 personnes

Construite au pied des pistes de la station et des remontées mécaniques, la résidence de style pyrénéen marie harmonieusement les matériaux traditionnels de la région: le bois, la pierre et l'ardoise. Tous les services sont regroupés au rez-de-chaussée.

Le confort
Équipement commun à tous les types : séjour, coin-cuisine, équipé (plaques, réfrigérateur), salle de bains/wc.
- Appartement 2 pièces 4 personnes: 25 m² environ, séjour avec 2 lits simples, chambre avec 2 lits simples ou 2 lits superposés.
- Appartements 3 pièces 6 personnes: 35m² environ, séjour avec 2 lits simples, chambre

avec 2 lits simples ou 2 lits superposés, seconde chambre avec grand lit ou 2 lits simples.
- Appartement 4 pièces duplex 8 personnes: 45 m² environ, séjour avec 2 lits simples, chambre avec 2 lits simples ou 2 lits superposés; à l'étage, 2 chambres avec chacune 2 lits simples ou 2 lits superposés.

A votre disposition
Réception, bar, restaurant, location de linge de literie et de toilette (14€/personne/semaine), lit bébé (25,50€/semaine), TV (36,80€/semaine). Animaux acceptés (25,50€/animal/semaine).

Formule de séjour
Location simple (draps non fournis).

a Underline in the text the words for each of the following:
price
ski-lifts
wood, stone and slate
on the ground floor
kitchenette
hot-plates, refrigerator
living room with two single beds
bunk beds
upstairs
hire of bed-linen and towels
sheets not provided

b On which floor will you find the bar and restaurant? _____

c Are pets accepted? _____

d Roughly what is the surface area of one of the two-roomed apartments? _____

e Which is the only type of flat in which you might find a double bed? _____

Answers p. 32
f How much does it cost to hire a cot? _____

9 On the recording, Jean-Pierre will ask you about your recent skiing holiday. You will need to recycle the language from Conversation 3 for your replies.

KEY WORDS AND PHRASES

je suis resté(e) à Toulouse	I stayed in Toulouse
je suis parti(e) au mois d'août	I went off in the month of August
je suis revenu(e) à Toulouse	I came back to Toulouse
au-dessus du Portugal	above (i.e. north of) Portugal
pas moderne, très archaïque	not modern, very archaic
sauvage, magnifique	wild, magnificent
une dizaine de jours	about ten days
dix copains à moi	ten friends of mine
dix copines à moi	ten (female) friends of mine
mon copain/ma copine	my boyfriend/my girlfriend
on s'est baigné	we bathed
on a passé un bon moment	we had a good time
comment s'est passé le voyage?	how did the trip go?
tu es parti(e) quand?	when did you go?
pendant une semaine	for a week
un petit peu moins touristique	a little bit less touristic
un petit peu plus compliqué	a little bit more complicated
Je suis resté(e) là-bas	I stayed there
en fin de compte	in the end
les vieux quartiers historiques	the old historical districts
de toute façon	in any case
comment va-t-elle?	how is she?
comment vas-tu?	how are you?
comment allez-vous?	how are you?
elle s'est cassé quelque chose	she has broken something
elle s'est retourné le pied	she twisted her foot
je me suis cassé le bras	I have broken my arm
se faire mal	to hurt oneself
partir au ski	to go skiing
un meilleur niveau	a better level
par contre	on the other hand
elle n'a pas de chance	she is unlucky

The perfect with être

The following verbs and their compounds form their perfect with **être**. Apart from reflexive verbs, they are the only verbs to do so. In other words, when you have learned this list, you know them all.

Infinitive		*Perfect*
aller	to go	**je suis allé(e)** etc.
venir	to come	**je suis venu(e)**
arriver	to arrive	**je suis arrivé(e)**
partir	to leave	**je suis parti(e)**
entrer	to enter	**je suis entré(e)**
sortir	to go out	**je suis sorti(e)**
monter	to go up	**je suis monté(e)**
descendre	to go down	**je suis descendu(e)**
rester	to stay	**je suis resté(e)**
tomber	to fall	**je suis tombé(e)**
retourner	to return	**je suis retourné(e)**
naître	to be born	**je suis né(e)**
mourir	to die	**il est mort/elle est morte**

Mort/morte is the only one of these past participles where there is a difference in pronunciation between the masculine and the feminine: in the masculine the 't' of **mort** is not pronounced: in the feminine **morte** it is pronounced.

10   When you have learned that list, cover it up and see if you can write out the perfect for **on** (which counts as masculine singular). The first one has been done for you.

aller	**on est allé**
venir	_____
arriver	_____
partir	_____
entrer	_____
sortir	_____
monter	_____
descendre	_____
rester	_____
tomber	_____
retourner	_____
naître	_____
mourir	_____

| Answers p. 32 |

11 In the passage below, some of the verbs in brackets form their perfect with **être** and some with **avoir**. See if you can fill in the correct forms for a male speaker.

Nous [aller] _____ _____ en Corse cette année. C'était assez

compliqué. Nous [partir] _____ _____ de Paris en avion à dix

heures du matin. Nous [arriver] _____ _____ à Marseille une

heure plus tard. De l'aéroport de Marseille-Marignane, nous [prendre] _____

_____ un car pour aller jusqu'au port. Nous [faire] _____

_____ la traversée en bateau et puis nous [attendre] _____

_____ un bus pour aller jusqu'à notre village. C'est à sept heures du soir

seulement que nous [monter] _____ _____ dans l'appartement.

> Answers p. 32

The perfect of a reflexive verb

se lever, to get up:

je me suis levé(e)	**nous nous sommes levé(e)s**
tu t'es levé(e)	**vous vous êtes levé(e)(s)**
il s'est levé	**ils se sont levés**
elle s'est levée	**elles se sont levées**

Again, in the negative, **ne** and **pas** go either side of the bit of **être**, e.g. **je ne me suis pas levé(e), tu ne t'es pas levé(e).**

Note: One verb which does <u>not</u> form its perfect tense with **être** is the verb 'to be': **être** itself. As you saw in Unit 1, the perfect of **être** is formed with **avoir**: **j'ai été** 'I have been', **nous avons été** 'we have been', etc.

12 Fill in the gaps with the perfect tense of the verbs indicated. The form given in brackets is the usual infinitive with **se**, but you will need to replace the **se** with **me, nous** or whatever is appropriate. Assume any ambiguous gender to be masculine.

a   Hier soir, nous [se coucher] _____ très tard.

b   C'est ainsi que ça [se faire] _____

c   A quelle heure est-ce que vous [se lever] _____, Monsieur?

d   Qu'est-ce qui [se passer] _____?

e   Je [se trouver] _____ sans argent.

f   Est-ce que tu [se laver] _____?

> Answers p. 32

Names of countries

The names of countries are generally very similar in French and English, so you will usually be understood if you say the English name with a French accent!

The majority of country names are feminine and are preceded by **en** when you talk about going there:

Il est parti en Belgique	He went off to Belgium
Elle est allée en Nouvelle-Zélande	She went to New Zealand

However, there are some country names which are masculine. (For some reason, both North and South America have masculine tendencies!) The list of masculine countries on this page is not exhaustive, but it is a fair rule of thumb to assume that any country not on it is most likely to be feminine.

With masculine country names, you don't use **en** but **au** (or, of course, **à l'** or **aux**):

Ils sont allés au Brésil	They went to Brazil
Il est parti à l'Angola	He went off to Angola
Elle est partie aux États-Unis	She went off to the United States

Masculine names of countries

le Portugal
le Canada
les États-Unis
le Mexique
le Venezuela
le Brésil
le Paraguay
l'Uruguay
le Pérou
le Chili
le Japon
le Viêt-nam
le Pakistan
l'Angola
le Niger
le Tchad
le Soudan
le Zimbabwe

13 Write out a dozen sentences saying where you have and have not been. Try to ring the changes between:

Je suis (déjà) allé(e)...
Je ne suis pas (encore) allé(e)... ⎫ ...**en** (+ feminine country name)
Pendant les vacances, je suis parti(e)... ⎬ ...**au/à l'/aux** (+ masculine country name)
J'ai fait un voyage... ⎭

It would be worth looking up in a dictionary and trying to learn the names and genders of countries which are of interest to you.

14

Looking at the map below, imagine that you have travelled

- from Saint-Martin to Piquefort
- from Rive-en-Val to Challand-les-Forges
- from Cantou to Montfernand
- from Merville to Paris

Working aloud, give the details of your journeys: e.g.

Je suis parti(e) de...
J'ai pris le train/le bus/le car (coach) **jusqu'à...**
J'ai changé à...
Je suis allé(e) à... en avion/en voiture/en train/en bus/à pied
J'ai laissé la voiture à...
J'ai marché jusqu'à...
J'ai continué jusqu'à...
J'ai traversé...
Je suis arrivé(e) à...

Jean-Pierre and Marianne give some possible answers on the recording. When you have listened to them, try giving an account of the same or different journeys in which you speak in the plural (**Nous sommes parti(e)s**, etc.).

If you are working with a partner, take it in turns to recount a journey to the other person – and be prepared to answer their questions about it.

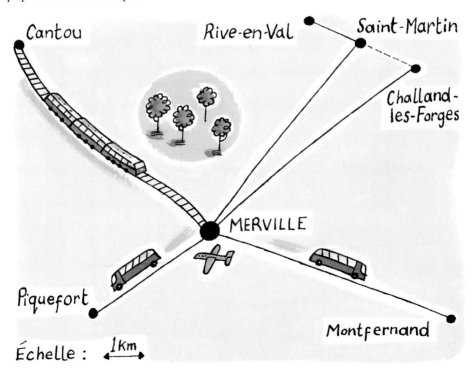

EXERCISE 1

(a) an island (in an ocean of rainforest) **(b)** the gold rush **(c)** by plane **(d)** about 100

EXERCISE 2

(a) nous sommes allés / nous sommes rentrés / un bébé singe est né / nous sommes arrivés / nous sommes retournés / nous sommes repartis / nous y sommes restés / nous sommes aussi sortis / qui sont tous venus nous voir

EXERCISE 4

(a) A man, because of the masculine form of allé and other past participles **(b)** Last June **(c)** Two hours **(d)** Jean-Claude **(e)** At a hotel in the centre of town **(f)** Three or four days **(g)** She went back to England **(h)** He went to stay with Jean-Claude **(i)** Three days **(j)** They talked about their work **(k)** Their new project was born

EXERCISE 5

(a) Saint Petersburg **(b)** Plane **(c)** Jean-Pierre's hotel **(d)** Magnificent **(e)** Six (from 11 a.m. to 5 p.m.) **(f)** Two days later **(g)** One week

EXERCISE 7

la cheville / le bras / le poignet / l'orteil

EXERCISE 8

(a) prix / remontées mécaniques / le bois, la pierre et l'ardoise / au rez-de-chaussée / coin-cuisine / plaques, réfrigérateur / séjour avec deux lits simples / lits superposés / à l'étage / location de linge de literie et de toilette / draps non fournis **(b)** Ground floor (All the amenities are together on the ground floor: Tous les services sont regroupés au rez-de-chaussée.) **(c)** Yes (Animaux acceptés) **(d)** 25 m² **(e)** Some of the three-roomed apartments **(f)** 25.50€ per week

EXERCISE 10

on est allé / on est venu / on est arrivé / on est parti / on est entré / on est sorti / on est monté / on est descendu / on est resté / on est tombé / on est retourné / on est né / on est mort

EXERCISE 11

sommes allés / sommes partis / sommes arrivés / avons pris / avons fait / avons attendu / sommes montés

EXERCISE 12

(a) Hier soir, nous nous sommes couchés trés tard. **(b)** C'est ainsi que ça s'est fait. **(c)** A quelle heure est-ce que vous vous êtes levé, Monsieur? **(d)** Qu'est-ce qui s'est passé? **(e)** Je me suis trouvé sans argent. **(f)** Est-ce que tu t'es lavé?

3

THE WAY
IT WAS

**WHAT YOU
WILL LEARN**

- ► expressing thanks
- ► understanding descriptions of the past
- ► talking about how things used to be
- ► using the imperfect tense
- ► some expressions of time

**POINTS TO
REMEMBER**

The perfect tense is used to recount actions which took place in the past. In Units 1 and 2 you met the two ways of forming it:

- **j'ai travaillé**, **tu as travaillé**, **il a travaillé**, etc. (the pattern followed by most verbs)
- **je suis allé(e)**, **tu es allé(e)**, **il est allé**, etc. (the pattern followed by the handful of so-called verbs of motion)

**BEFORE YOU
BEGIN**

This unit introduces another tense, called the imperfect – which doesn't imply that there is anything wrong with it! Whereas the perfect tense is used of actions (e.g. he came in), the imperfect is used for description (e.g. he was happy), for habitual actions (e.g. she used to come in every morning) or to convey the notion of continuation (e.g. they were working). There will be more explanation in the Grammar section.

The imperfect is a great deal easier to master than the perfect, because the endings are absolutely regular – even for the verb **être**!
They are: **-ais, -ais, -ait,** -**ait, -ions, -iez, -aient, -aient**. For example, the imperfect of the verb **avoir** looks like this:

j'avais	**nous avions**
tu avais	**vous aviez**
il avait	**ils avaient**
elle avait	**elles avaient**

The endings **-ais, -ait** and **-aient** all sound the same.

Matthieu telephones to thank his hostess

Matthieu

Oui, bonjour – c'est
Matthieu...Oui, je vous
appelais pour...pour la
soirée de samedi soir
dernier...pour vous
remercier tout d'abord de

LISTEN FOR...

these examples of the imperfect tense:

je vous appelais	I was calling you
je voulais vous dire	I wanted to tell you
votre repas était très, très bon	your meal was very, very good
je vous téléphonais	I was telephoning you

m'avoir invité...et parce que j'ai passé une soirée merveilleuse...Oui...Je, je
voulais vous dire que votre repas était très, très bon – j'ai adoré la
bavette...et...j'ai beaucoup aimé ensuite qu'on soit tous partis au concert dans
l'église. Je vous remercie beaucoup, hein, franchement...c'était très, très beau,
hein, très, très intéressant...Mm mm...Mm mm. Oui...Je vous téléphonais
surtout pour...pour vous donner un grand merci et...Oui...En tout cas, merci
beaucoup...Au revoir.

VOCABULARY

merveilleux, -euse	marvellous
le repas	meal
la bavette	sirloin
franchement	frankly, honestly

je vous appelais I was calling you. This is
from the imperfect tense of the verb
appeler. The Grammar section will explain
further.

la soirée de samedi soir dernier the evening
we spent together last Saturday evening.
Une soirée is what goes on socially in the
course of **un soir** – it can mean a reception
or party. **La soirée de samedi** would have
been a simpler way of putting it, but natural
speech is sometimes convoluted.

pour vous remercier...de in order to thank
you for...The basic construction is
remercier quelqu'un de quelque chose:
**Je vous remercie beaucoup de votre
lettre**.

de m'avoir invité for inviting me (literally for
me to have invited). **Avoir invité** is in the
past, because the inviting took place before
the thanking. French often uses an
infinitive where English has a form in -ing:
Merci d'être venu 'Thanks for coming.'

Note too that the pronouns **me, te, se,
nous, vous, le, la, les, lui, leur, y** and **en**
come in front of the whole verb, including
the infinitive: **Nous vous remercions de
nous avoir envoyé ces belles photos**
'Thank you for sending us these beautiful
photos.'

était was. From the imperfect of **être**.

qu'on soit tous partis au concert that we all
went off to the concert. In certain
constructions, **que** is followed by a form of
the verb called the subjunctive: in this case,
soit, from the verb **être**. However, this is a
refinement which you do not need to use
yourself at this stage.

En tout cas Anyway (literally in any case).

PRACTICE

1

a If Matthieu had written to thank his hostess rather than telephoning her, what would be the words in the gaps below? If you're stuck, the missing words are in the box.

était	merci	invité	remercie	église	soirée

> *Chère Madame,*
>
> *Je vous _____ beaucoup de la*
>
> *_____ de samedi. C'est vraiment gentil*
>
> *de m'avoir _____ Votre dîner*
>
> *_____ délicieux – surtout la bavette – et*
>
> *j'ai beaucoup aimé le concert dans l'_____*
>
> *Pour tout, un très, très grand _____ !*
>
> *Avec mon meilleur souvenir,*
>
> *Matthieu*

b Jean-Pierre says those missing words on the recording. You can give yourself some pronunciation practice by repeating them after him – the sounds [r], [é] and [i] are the ones to concentrate on.

Answers p. 48

2

Many French city-dwellers have a second home, **une résidence secondaire**, in the country, in the mountains or by the sea. They quite often invite friends to stay with them there. On the recording, Marianne telephones to thank her hostess for this kind of hospitality. Listen as many times as you like and see if you can tell:

a What was the name of the village?

☐ Saint-Martin ☐ Saint-Georges ☐ Saint-Malo

b How long was Marianne there?

☐ two weeks ☐ a week ☐ a weekend

c Was she staying in

☐ a flat? ☐ a house? ☐ a caravan?

d Was it

☐ quiet? ☐ noisy? ☐ or doesn't she say?

e Is the village

☐ in the Alps? ☐ in the Pyrenees? ☐ in the Massif Central?

f How keen is Marianne on going for mountain walks?

Answers p. 48

☐ not keen ☐ reasonably keen ☐ very keen

3 Working with parallel texts (i.e. with the translation alongside the French) is an excellent way of building up your reading skills.

In **La jeune fille au pair**, written by Joseph Joffo and set in 1950, the heroine works as an au pair for a Jewish family as she struggles to come to terms with the knowledge that her loving father was a Nazi war criminal. This paragraph from the novel evokes her rose-tinted image of her childhood:

Il était une fois une grande maison de pierre meulière au milieu d'un grand jardin fleuri de roses, de tulipes et de bégonias. L'été, on y piqueniquait à l'ombre de chênes centenaires. L'hiver, on se réunissait devant la cheminée du salon, surmontée des trophées de chasse de Papa et, tout en contemplant un gai feu de bois, on écoutait l'un des disques de Maman. Le gramophone égrenait tour à tour aussi bien du Beethoven que du Strauss, Gershwin ou Zarah Leander. Bien calé dans son fauteuil de brocart, Papa levait de temps en temps la tête de son livre ou de son journal pour mieux sourire à sa femme et à ses enfants, un petit garçon et une petite fille blonde aux yeux clairs, comme leurs parents.	Once upon a time, there was a big house of buhrstone in the middle of a big garden full of roses, tulips and begonias. In summer, they used to picnic there, in the shade of hundred-year-old oaks. In winter, they gathered in front of the fireplace of the sitting-room, which had Daddy's hunting trophies above it, and, staring into a gay wood fire, they would listen to one of Mummy's records. The gramophone gave out in turn as readily Beethoven as Strauss, Gershwin or Zarah Leander. Well ensconced in his brocade armchair, Daddy from time to time raised his head from his book or newspaper the better to smile at his wife and his children, a little boy and a little girl who was blond with light-coloured eyes, like their parents.

(©Editors Jean-Claude Lattès 1993)

a Go through the paragraph underlining the six verbs in the imperfect.

b Answer in French; there is no need for full sentences:

i. **Où piqueniquait-on en été?**

_____

ii. **Où est-ce que la famille se réunissait en hiver?**

_____

iii. **Qu'est-ce qui surmontait la cheminée?**

_____

iv. **Qu'est-ce qu'on faisait, tout en contemplant le feu de bois?**

_____

v. **A qui Papa souriait-il?**

_____

vi. **Comment était la petite fille?**

Answers p. 48

_____

CONVERSATION 2

Yves reminisces about his childhood in Algeria

Yves

Je suis né en Algérie, dans une petite ville près d'Alger, Boufarik, et, l'été, c'était très humide et c'était très dur d'y rester, et mes parents m'envoyaient au bord de la mer, chez mes grands-parents à Philippeville (maintenant ça s'appelle Skigda), vers la frontière tunisienne. Alors là, je..., ma grand-mère m'amenait à la plage au début, en autobus, tous les matins; j'y passais trois heures à regarder les poissons dans les rochers avec un masque et un tuba, et ensuite, à midi, elle me servait...ce qu'elle appelait un quinquina, c'est-à-dire un mélange de vin de table rouge ordinaire et d'un extrait d'herbes aromatiques, la quintonine, vendue en pharmacie, peut-être encore maintenant.

VOCABULARY

l'Algérie (f.)	Algeria
humide	humid
la frontière	border
tunisien(ne)	Tunisian
amener	to take (someone somewhere)
le rocher	rock
le masque	mask
le tuba	snorkel

Je suis né en Algérie   I was born in Algeria. **Naître** (to be born) is one of the verbs which form their perfect tense with **être**, as you saw in the Grammar section of Unit 2. French people born in Algeria are colloquially known as **pieds-noirs**.

l'été   in summer. The text in Exercise 3 also contained an example of **l'été** being used to mean in summer, as opposed to just the summer. However, you can also say **en été**.

c'était très dur d'y rester   it was very hard to stay there.

mes parents m'envoyaient au bord de la mer   my parents used to send me to the seaside. The verb (from **envoyer**) is in the imperfect because this is something Yves's parents did every year.

maintenant ça s'appelle Skigda   now it's called Skigda. Learn also **Ça s'appelle comment**? 'What's it called?'

ma grand-mère m'amenait à la plage au début, en autobus, tous les matins   my grandmother used to take me to the beach at the beginning, by bus, every morning (literally, all the mornings). Again, the verb (this time from **amener**) is in the imperfect because this is something the grandmother did repeatedly.

j'y passais trois heures à regarder les poissons   I used to spend three hours there watching the fish.

ce qu'elle appelait un quinquina   what (literally that which) she called a quinine tonic wine. He goes on to explain what this was.

c'est-à-dire un mélange de vin de table rouge ordinaire et d'un extrait d'herbes aromatiques, la quintonine   that is to say, a mixture of ordinary red table wine and an extract of aromatic herbs [called] quintonine.

PRACTICE

4 Not all French children are allowed to drink wine. Jean-Pierre wasn't – except for one disastrous occasion when his aunt let him have some mulled wine (**du vin chaud**). Hear all about it on the recording!

You'll find it helps to listen to the recording several times before you try to write the missing verbs in the gaps in the transcript below. Take particular care over the spelling, since, although **-ais**, **-ait** and **-aient** all sound the same, they are not interchangeable in writing.

Quand j'_____ petit, je n'avais absolument pas le droit de boire du vin, mais

j'en _____ vraiment envie, parce que c'était quelque chose qui était réservé

aux grandes personnes. Mes parents m' _____ assez souvent chez une vieille

tante. Or, une fois en hiver, cette tante avait

une dizaine d'invités à la maison. Il

_____ très froid dehors,

alors elle a préparé un vin chaud. Pour elle, un

vin chaud, ce n'_____ pas

de l'alcool, alors j'ai eu le droit d'en boire. Moi,

j'ai trouvé que c'_____ très

bon: c'était sucré, comme une boisson

d'enfant. Alors, pendant que ma tante et les

invités se _____ au salon,

moi je me _____ du vin chaud dans la cuisine. Lorsque ma tante est venue

dans la cuisine, elle m'a trouvé complètement soûl. J'ai dormi pendant quatorze heures et, le

lendemain, j'_____ vraiment mal à la tête – et je n'avais absolument plus envie

de boire du vin comme les grandes personnes!

Answers p. 48

5 On the recording, Jean-Pierre asks you about your childhood (**l'enfance**). Follow Philippe's prompts to paint an idyllic picture. All but one of the verbs you will need to use came in Conversation 2: **je suis né(e), je passais, (mes parents) m'envoyaient, (mon grand-père) m'amenait, nous allions, c'était.**

6 See if you can follow this extract from an article in *l'Express* well enough to answer the questions below – you won't need to understand every word to do so..

'L'Algérie n'est pas la France, la France n'est pas l'Algérie.'...

La France n'est certes pas l'Algérie, mais 700.000 Algériens vivent sur son territoire, ainsi qu'un million de binationaux, sans compter un nombre par définition inconnu de clandestins...Il faut ajouter au tableau les survivants et descendants du million de pieds-noirs rapatriés en 1962, et les 2 millions d'appelés qui, durant les 'événements' ont effectué leur service militaire (jusqu'à trente mois) en Algérie. Une population importante, donc, pour laquelle l'Algérie reste une blessure...

VOCABULARY	
le clandestin	illegal immigrant
l'appelé (m.)	conscript
les événements (m.)	troubles (literally events)
la blessure	wound

a   How many Algerians live in France? _____

b   How many people in France have French–Algerian dual nationality?

_____

c   What figure is described as 'unknown by definition'?

_____

d   How many French people were repatriated from Algeria in 1962?

_____

e   How many Frenchmen did their military service in Algeria during the 'troubles'? _____

f   What was the maximum length of a period of military service there?

Answers p. 48   _____

The old hospitals of Toulouse

Guide

Nous sommes ici sur la rive droite de la Garonne et nous avons de l'autre côté du fleuve le quartier Saint-Cyprien qui, depuis le moyen âge, accueille les

LISTEN FOR...	
la rive droite de la Garonne	the right bank of the Garonne
le quartier Saint-Cyprien	the Saint-Cyprien district
accueille	welcomes
des lits collectifs	communal beds
un cimetière	a cemetery

malades, hein, les personnes âgées, les mendiants, dans deux hôpitaux qui ont été construits entre le douzième et le quatorzième siècle. Ces malades mangeaient dans de grands réfectoires, qui étaient au bord de l'eau; ils dormaient dans de grands dortoirs dans des lits collectifs, où ils partageaient la couche avec deux ou trois personnes. Ils étaient soignés par des médecins et ils étaient également enterrés dans un cimetière que nous avons conservé jusqu'à une date récente.

VOCABULARY

le/la malade	sick person, patient
le réfectoire	refectory
le dortoir	dormitory
enterré (from **enterrer**)	buried

nous avons de l'autre côté du fleuve we have on the other side of the river. **Un fleuve** is bigger than **une rivière**.

qui, depuis le moyen âge, accueille les malades, les personnes âgées, les mendiants which, since the Middle Ages, has taken in the sick, the elderly, beggars. Because it still takes them in today, **accueille** (from the verb **accueillir**) is in the present tense. Similarly: **Nous habitons ici depuis dix ans** 'We have lived here for ten years' (and we still do).

deux hôpitaux qui ont été construits entre le douzième et le quatorzième siècle two hospitals which were built between the twelfth and the fourteenth centuries. The singular is **un hôpital**.

mangeaient used to eat. A note for the eagle-eyed: when the letter **g** is followed by **e** or **i**, it is pronounced 'soft', like **je**. When it is followed by **a**, **o** or **u**, it is pronounced 'hard', as in **gaga**. All of the parts of

manger are pronounced soft; this is shown in writing by inserting an **e** between the **g** and any ending beginning with **a** or **o** – there aren't any beginning with **u**. So 'we eat' is **nous mangeons** and the imperfect has the forms **je mangeais** but nous **mangions**. The same pattern applies to the verb **partager** below.

où ils partageaient la couche where they shared the bed. Linked to **se coucher** 'to go to bed': **Je me couche tôt** 'I go to bed early.'

Ils étaient soignés par des médecins they were looked after by doctors. **Soigner** is to look after or to nurse: **Les médecins soignaient les malades** 'Doctors used to look after the patients.'

PRACTICE

7 Can you write out the French words for the following? Look back at the Conversation if you need to – you'll find them all there. Use **les** before each of the plural nouns.

doctors _____

sick people _____

old people _____

hospitals _____

a cemetery _____

a dormitory _____

Answers p. 48
a refectory _____

*The **Pont Neuf**, which crosses the **Garonne** to the*
quartier Saint-Cyprien

8 Marianne spent some of her childhood at a boarding school. She talks about it on the recording. The words you may not know include: **des pensionnaires** (not 'pensioners', but 'boarders'), **loin de** 'far from', **seul(e)** 'alone' and **on avait intérêt à ne pas...** 'it was in your interests not to...'. Listen and see if you can answer the following questions:

a Why were most of the pupils boarding?

_____

b What was Marianne's reason for boarding?

_____

_____

c How many people were there in the refectory? _____

_____

d How many people slept in each room in the dormitories? _____

e Why did Marianne sleep badly?

_____

f Whom does she describe as a dragon? _____

g What was Marianne's one desire while she was at school?

Answers p. 48

_____

9 Working with the recording, tell Jean-Pierre about the time you were in hospital. Your part includes the following:

je me couchais / je dormais mal / il y avait / la salle (= room or ward) **/ on nous réveillait / était / je prenais une douche / je parlais aux autres malades**

KEY WORDS
AND PHRASES

je vous appelais	I was calling you
la soirée de samedi	Saturday evening
tout d'abord	first of all
pour vous remercier	in order to thank you
de m'avoir invité(e)	for having invited me
j'ai passé	I spent
une soirée merveilleuse	a marvellous evening
je voulais vous dire que	I wanted to tell you that
votre repas était très bon	your meal was very good
je vous remercie beaucoup	thank you very much
c'était très beau	it was really lovely
je vous téléphonais surtout	I was phoning you above all
pour vous donner	to say (literally to give you)
un grand merci	a big thank you
je suis né(e) en Algérie	I was born in Algeria
l'été, c'était très humide	in the summer, it was very humid
c'était très dur d'y rester	it was hard to stay there
mes parents m'envoyaient	my parents used to send me
au bord de la mer	to the seaside
ma grand-mère m'amenait	my grandmother used to take me
à la plage	to the beach
tous les matins,	every morning,
j'y passais trois heures	I spent three hours there
à regarder les poissons	looking at the fish
avec un masque et un tuba	with a mask and snorkel
la rive droite/gauche	the right/left bank
de l'autre côté du fleuve	on the other side of the river
depuis le moyen âge	since the Middle Ages
les hôpitaux	the hospitals
accueillent	have welcomed
les malades	the sick
les personnes âgées	the elderly
les mendiants	beggars
l'hôpital a été construit	the hospital was built
entre le douzième	between the twelfth
et le quatorzième siècle	and the fourteenth centuries
ils mangeaient	they used to eat
dans de grands réfectoires	in big refectories
ils dormaient	they used to sleep
dans de grands dortoirs	in big dormitories
ils étaient soignés	they were looked after
par des médecins	by doctors
ils étaient enterrés	they were buried
dans un cimetière	in a cemetery
jusqu'à une date récente	until recently

GRAMMAR AND EXERCISES

The imperfect tense

- The imperfect tense paints the background:
  It <u>was</u> a lovely sunny day; the sun <u>was shining</u>; the birds <u>were singing</u>; etc.
- It translates 'used to':
  The old man <u>used to have</u> his breakfast in the café every morning.
- It is also used to describe what was going on at the time that some event took place:
  The procession <u>was working its way</u> up the Champs-Élysées when someone let off a fire-cracker.
  The perfect is used for specific actions that take place against the backdrop painted by the
  imperfect (in this example, 'someone let off a fire-cracker').

The endings of the imperfect are: **-ais, -ais, -ait, -ait, -ions, -iez, -aient, -aient**. But what about the
beginning of the verb – the stem? Except in the case of **être**, it is the **nous** form of the present tense
minus the **-ons** ending. Examples:

Infinitive	Present tense	Imperfect tense
danser	nous <u>dans</u>ons	je dansais...nous dansions...etc.
vendre	nous <u>vend</u>ons	je vendais...nous vendions...etc.
prendre	nous <u>pren</u>ons	je prenais...nous prenions...etc.
faire	nous <u>fais</u>ons	je faisais...nous faisions...etc.
finir	nous <u>finiss</u>ons	je finissais...nous finissions...etc.
venir	nous <u>ven</u>ons	je venais...nous venions...etc.

The one irregular stem is that for **être**, where it is **ét-**:

j'étais	nous étions
tu étais	vous étiez
il était	ils étaient
elle était	elles étaient

10 To help you learn the forms, write out the whole of the imperfect tense of the verb **faire**.
(We make/We do is **nous faisons**.)

je	_faisais_	nous	_____
tu	_____	vous	_____
il	_____	ils	_____
elle	_____	elles	_____

The spelling is perfectly regular, but the pronunciation is
probably not what you would expect, so the answer to this
exercise is given on the recording as well as on p. 48.

Answers p. 48

11 See if you can fill in the form of the imperfect indicated for each of the following verbs:

être	nous	_____
tenir	il	_____
vouloir	tu	_____
avoir	vous	_____
prendre	elle	_____
dormir	il	_____
téléphoner	vous	_____
passer	ils	_____
servir	nous	_____
apprendre	elles	_____

Answers p. 48

12 Try to fill in the correct form of the imperfect tense for each of the verbs in brackets.

Quand j'[être] _____ enfant, mes grands-parents [habiter] _____
au bord de la mer. C'[être] _____ à deux heures de chez nous, alors mes parents
m'y amenaient assez souvent. En général, nous y [rester] _____ quelques jours:
l'été, on [aller] _____ à la plage et on se baignait; l'hiver, on se réunissait devant
la cheminée: on [parler] _____ , on [jouer] _____ , on [regarder]
_____ la télévision. Le soir, quand je me couchais, ma grand-mère [venir]
_____ dans ma chambre et elle me lisait des livres d'enfants – j'[adorer]
_____ ça.

Answers p. 48

Other expressions of time

See how many of these you already know:

maintenant	now
aujourd'hui	today
hier	yesterday
hier soir	yesterday evening
demain	tomorrow
toujours	always, still
souvent	often
puis	then, next
ensuite	then, next
alors	well then, at that time
à cette époque	at that time
samedi soir	Saturday evening (past or future)
le samedi soir	on Saturday evening<u>s</u>
le samedi	on Saturdays
tous les matins	every morning
tous les soirs	every evening
tous les jours	every day
un an	a year
six mois	six months
l'année dernière	last year
l'été/en été	in summer
l'hiver/en hiver	in winter
à midi	at midday
à minuit	at midnight
au quatorzième siècle	in the fourteenth century
au moyen âge	in the Middle Ages

13 You will need to use the imperfect and one of the expressions of time from that list to translate each of the following into French. Looking back at the Conversations will help if you get stuck. For the sake of simplicity, take 'you' as = **vous**.

a Your meal was very good yesterday evening.

_____

b I used to telephone you every evening.

_____

c Yves used to go to the beach every morning.

_____

d He used to spend three hours there every day.

_____

e In summer, you used to play in the water.

_____

f We used to picnic at midday.

_____

_____

Answers p. 48

14 **a** See if you can prepare some questions for interviewing someone about his or her childhood. Your questions might begin:

Est-ce que vous _____?

Où est-ce que vous _____?

Quand est-ce que vous _____?

Comment est-ce que vous _____?

Pourquoi est-ce que vous _____?

Avec qui est-ce que vous _____?

Remember that you will need to use the imperfect for habitual actions and the perfect for one-off events.

When you have worked out your questions, you can play a game of Consequences with the recording: with the pause button on, ask a question, then release the pause button and listen to Marianne's answer... which may or may not make sense!

b Plan how you would answer those questions yourself. Feel free to be imaginative rather than accurate!

c If you are working with a partner, you can take turns to interview each other along the lines each of you has prepared.

ANSWERS

EXERCISE 1

remercie / soirée / invité / était / église / merci

EXERCISE 2

(a) Saint-Martin   **(b)** a weekend   **(c)** a house
(d) quiet   **(e)** in the Pyrenees   **(f)** very keen

EXERCISE 3

(a) était / piqueniquait / (se) réunissait / écoutait /
égrenait / levait   **(b)** i. dans le jardin OR à l'ombre
de chênes centenaires   ii. devant la cheminée du
salon   iii. les trophées de chasse de Papa   iv. on
écoutait l'un des disques de Maman   v. à sa femme
et à ses enfants   vi. blonde aux yeux clairs

EXERCISE 4

étais / avais / amenaient / faisait / était / était /
parlaient / servais / avais

EXERCISE 6

(a) 700,000   **(b)** 1 million   **(c)** The number of
illegal immigrants   **(d)** 1 million   **(e)** 2 million
(f) 30 months

EXERCISE 7

les médecins / les malades / les personnes âgées /
les hôpitaux / un cimetière / un dortoir / un réfectoire

EXERCISE 8

(a) Their parents were diplomats who had gone
abroad.   **(b)** She lived in the country, too far from the
school to make the return journey every day.
(c) 300   **(d)** 10–12   **(e)** You could never be alone
and she didn't like that.   **(f)** The school nurse.
(g) To go home for the holidays.

EXERCISE 10

je faisais / tu faisais / il faisait / elle faisait / nous
faisions / vous faisiez / ils faisaient / elles faisaient

EXERCISE 11

nous étions / il tenait / tu voulais / vous aviez / elle
prenait / il dormait / vous téléphoniez / ils passaient /
nous servions / elles apprenaient

EXERCISE 12

étais / habitaient / était / restions / allait / parlait /
jouait / regardait / venait / adorais

EXERCISE 13

(a) Votre repas était très bon hier soir.   **(b)** Je vous
téléphonais tous les soirs.   **(c)** Yves allait à la plage
tous les matins.   **(d)** Il y passait trois heures tous
les jours.   **(e)** L'été/En été, vous jouiez dans l'eau.
(f) Nous piqueniquions /On piqueniquait à midi.

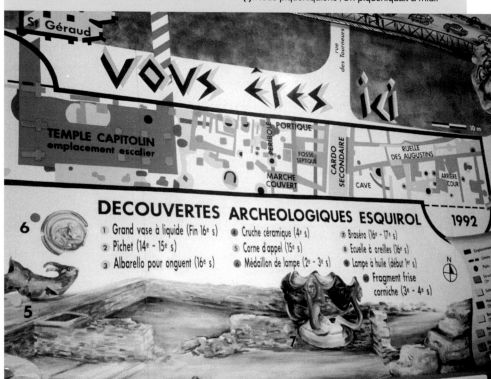

4 QUESTIONS AND ANSWERS

▶ understanding questions
▶ asking questions
▶ responding to questions

POINTS TO
REMEMBER

Units 1 and 2 looked at the main tense used for recounting past events – the perfect – and the two ways of forming it:

● with most verbs:
  j'ai, tu as, il a, etc. + the past participle (**travaillé, fini**, etc.)
● with the handful of so-called verbs of motion:
  je suis, tu es, il est, etc. + the past participle (**allé(e), parti(e)**, etc.)

Unit 3 then went on to the imperfect tense, which is used for describing things when talking about the past or for saying what used to happen. Its endings are:

● **-ais, -ais, -ait, -ait, -ions, -iez, -aient, -aient** (e.g. **j'allais, nous étions**)

BEFORE YOU
BEGIN

You'll be glad to hear that this unit doesn't introduce any new tenses. It focuses on asking questions and introduces 'inversion' as a way of forming them. Inversion means that the pronoun and the verb come in reverse order, e.g.

Vous êtes français.	You are French.
Etes-vous français?	Are you French?
Tu as lu le journal.	You have read the newspaper.
As-tu lu le journal?	Have you read the newspaper?

There will be more about this in the Grammar section.

One of the most important skills in coping with a foreign language is looking for clues and then not being afraid to guess at meanings. Many French words have some relation to English ones, even if they don't mean exactly the same as their counterparts. For instance, in Conversation 2, the new words include:

■ **le spectacle** – We'd say 'show', but the link with 'spectacle' gives a heavy clue.
■ **la scène** – Pierre says **la scène est petite**, which gives you a clue that the translation is not the obvious 'scene' – in fact, it is 'stage'.
■ **répéter** – You probably know this verb as meaning 'to repeat'. As the actors are going to 'repeat' the play before the performance, you can guess that it must mean 'to rehearse' in this context.

A matter of taste

Roger

C'est un fou qui marche dans le jardin de l'asile et il s'arrête devant un jardinier qui travaille et il lui dit: 'Qu'est-ce que vous faites, Monsieur?'

Il lui dit: 'Mais, mon ami, vous voyez: je mets du fumier sur les fraises!'

'Ah?' dit le fou, 'Pourquoi mettez-vous du fumier sur les fraises?'

'Pour qu'elles soient meilleures, mon ami!'

'Ah, oui!' dit le fou, 'Comme moi, je suis fou, je mets du sucre!'

LISTEN FOR...

un fou	madman
l'asile	asylum
un jardinier	gardener
du fumier	manure

VOCABULARY

marcher	to walk
le jardin	garden
s'arrêter	to stop
mon ami	my friend (here, patronising)
la fraise	strawberry
comme	(here) as, since

et lui dit and says to him. In another context, **lui** could mean 'to her'. **Dire** is 'to say' and **parler** 'to speak'.

Pourquoi mettez-vous du fumier sur les fraises? Why are you putting manure on the strawberries? Inversion can be used with question words (like **pourquoi**) as well as in yes/no questions. With **est-ce que...?**, the same question would be expressed **Pourquoi est-ce que vous mettez du fumier sur les fraises?**

Pour qu'elles soient meilleures So that they'll be better. Some expressions like **pour que** (so that) are followed by a form of the verb called the subjunctive, which you don't need to learn at this stage. **Soient** is from the subjunctive of the verb **être**. **Meilleures** ends in **-es** because **fraises** is feminine plural. The masculine singular form is **meilleur**: **Ce vin est meilleur que le beaujolais** 'This wine is better than beaujolais'; **Ce vin est le meilleur** 'This wine is the best.'

Comme moi, je suis fou As I'm mad. Adding **moi** emphasises 'I': **Moi, je préfère les pommes** '(I don't know about you, but) I prefer apples.'

PRACTICE

1 There is nothing calculated to destroy humour more than struggling to translate a joke, so it can be useful to have the odd funny story ready for use in French. The recording for this exercise breaks the story up into bite-sized chunks for you to repeat and learn by heart. Do your best to imitate Roger's pronunciation and intonation.

2 If you are confident that you know the French names of different kinds of fruit, cover up the left-hand column below and see if you can translate the words in the right-hand column, giving the genders as you do so. If you are less confident, you could try covering up the right-hand column and seeing which of the French names you can translate into English. And if you haven't a clue about the names of fruit – here's your chance to learn!

la fraise	strawberry
la framboise	raspberry
le cassis	blackcurrant
la mûre	blackberry
le raisin	grape
le pamplemousse	grapefruit
la pomme	apple
la pêche	peach
la prune	plum
l'abricot (m.)	apricot
la banane	banana
l'orange (f.)	orange
le fruit de la passion	passion-fruit

On the recording, you'll hear Jean-Pierre shopping for some of the fruit from that list. Write by the relevant item the quantity that he buys. **Une barquette** is a 'punnet'.

Answers p. 64

3 This questionnaire aims to measure one's stress level – and to give advice to the stressed-out.

avoir du mal	to have difficulty
déprimé(e)	depressed
se détendre	to relax
se réveiller	to wake up
boire ▷ (vous buvez)	to drink
Comment faites-vous?	How do you do it?

ETES-VOUS STRESSÉ(E)? RÉPONDEZ AUX QUESTIONS POUR VOIR...

a Avez-vous du mal à dormir?

OUI ☐ NON ☐

b Etes-vous toujours fatigué(e)?

OUI ☐ NON ☐

c Etes-vous déprimé(e)?

OUI ☐ NON ☐

d Avez-vous toujours trop de travail?

OUI ☐ NON ☐

e Refusez-vous souvent de sortir voir vos amis parce que vous n'avez pas le temps?

OUI ☐ NON ☐

f Avez-vous un sentiment de culpabilité si vous passez du temps à ne rien faire?

OUI ☐ NON ☐

g Quand vous partez en vacances, avez-vous du mal à vous détendre?

OUI ☐ NON ☐

h Quand vous êtes en vacances, pensez-vous beaucoup aux problèmes de la vie courante?

OUI ☐ NON ☐

i Avez-vous l'impression que les autres sont mieux organisés que vous?

OUI ☐ NON ☐

j Honnêtement, pensez-vous que vous buvez trop?

OUI ☐ NON ☐

INTERPRÉTATION

Donnez-vous 1 point pour chaque OUI...

Si vous avez 9–10 points...
OUI, vous êtes TRES stressé(e).

Si vous avez 5–8 points...
OUI, vous êtes stressé(e).

Alors...
Il faut essayer de vous simplifier la vie, de prendre du temps pour vous. Y a-t-il quelqu'un à qui vous pouvez parler de votre situation? Si vous travaillez plus de quarante heures par semaine, pouvez-vous dire à votre patron que c'en est trop? Essayez de faire de l'exercice au moins trois fois par semaine: il est difficile de trouver le temps, mais après, vous aurez plus d'énergie, alors tout ira plus vite. Allez faire des balades en respirant bien fort, partez en week-end de temps en temps, détendez-vous dans un bain moussant. N'oubliez pas l'importance des vitamines et des minéraux pour votre bien-être physique et psychologique. Et attention à l'alcool: en petites quantités ça vous détend et ça vous fait du bien – notamment au cœur – mais, si vous en abusez, vous serez encore plus déprimé(e) et encore plus fatigué(e) par la suite.

Si vous avez 2–4 points...
Vous êtes plutôt relax – comment faites-vous?

Si vous avez 0–1 points...
Comment vous êtes-vous réveillé(e) ce matin?

Amateur dramatics

Anne	Alors Pierre, où en es-tu avec la troupe de théâtre? Allez-vous bientôt jouer?
Pierre	Oui, nous jouons samedi soir – après-demain.
Anne	Où ça?
Pierre	Alors, à Toulouse, à côté de Toulouse, dans une petite ville, à Castelmaurou.
Anne	Mm mm. Et…comment ça se passe? Vous avez une salle adaptée?
Pierre	Non, enfin, c'est une salle qui est adaptée…pour le spectacle, mais c'est une salle de cinéma.
Anne	Comment, comment vous allez faire?
Pierre	Et, en fait, nous allons agrandir la scène, qui est très petite, et nous allons avoir des coulisses à l'extérieur de la salle.
Anne	Mais vous allez avoir froid!
Pierre	Oui, ça, sûrement, mais ça fait partie des risques du métier.
Anne	Mm. Vous pensez qu'il y a, qu'il va y avoir beaucoup de monde?
Pierre	On espère. A priori, on attend une centaine de personnes; le spectacle fonctionne bien actuellement.
Anne	Avez-vous fait la publicité?
Pierre	Oui, c'est la ville qui s'en est occupée. Il y a eu beaucoup de, d'affiches, de, de placardés, et ils ont aussi distribué des tracts.
Anne	Et allez-vous pouvoir répéter avant?
Pierre	Si tout va bien, nous répétons demain soir, dans les lieux du spectacle.

où en es-tu avec la troupe de théâtre? where are you at with the theatre group?

Allez-vous bientôt jouer? Are you going to put on a play soon? **Jouer** is normally 'to play': **jouer à** + a sport (**jouer au football**) and **jouer de** + an instrument (**jouer du piano**).

comment ça se passe? how does it work? **Se passer** is 'to happen'.

Vous avez une salle adaptée? Do you have a hall adapted [to your needs]? Anne calls Pierre **tu**, so the **vous** here is a plural, referring to the troupe.

ça fait partie des risques du métier that's part of the risks of the trade.

VOCABULARY

après-demain	the day after tomorrow
le spectacle	show
agrandir	enlarge
à l'extérieur	outside
le métier	trade, job
fonctionner	to function
actuellement	at the moment (not 'actually')
la publicité (also **la pub**)	publicity, advertising

Vous pensez qu'il y a, qu'il va y avoir beaucoup de monde? Do you think that there are, that there are going to be a lot of people?

A priori, on attend une centaine de personnes In principle, we're expecting about a hundred people. The Latin phrase 'a priori' is used more in French than in English. **Attendre** means 'to expect' as well as 'to wait for'.

c'est la ville qui s'en est occupée it's the town [council] which took care of it. **S'occuper de** means 'to take care of': **Je m'occupe des enfants** 'I'm taking care of the children.'

Il y a eu beaucoup […] d'affiches, […] de placardés, et ils ont aussi distribué des tracts There were a lot of posters and advertisements stuck up and they also distributed handbills. **Placarder** is to 'stick up a notice or poster'; **placardés** is the past participle, used here to mean 'things posted up' – in fact, it is another word for **affiches**.

allez-vous pouvoir répéter avant? will you be able to rehearse beforehand?

Si tout va bien If all goes well.

les lieux du spectacle the place where the show will be put on. **Le lieu** is 'place', but it is often used in the plural to mean 'premises'.

4 On the recording, Jean-Pierre asks Marianne about her next recording engagement, which turns out to be Racine's play *Andromaque*.

a   Where will the recording take place? _____

b   What role will Marianne be playing? _____

c   Is the recording for radio or television? _____

d   What other means of diffusion will it have? _____

e   How many days are allowed for rehearsal? _____

f   On which days will the recording take place? _____

Answers p. 64

g   When does Marianne think the play will be broadcast? _____

5 On the recording, Jean-Pierre asks you about your nephew (**votre neveu**) and his amateur dramatics. You will need the phrases

la grande salle hall (e.g. of a school)

chaque soir each evening

6 The Town Hall (le Capitole) of Toulouse houses a magnificent eighteenth-century theatre. The text below describes some of the work which goes on behind the scenes there.

VOCABULARY	
pleins feux sur...	spotlight on... (literally full lights on...)
le rayonnement	radiance, influence
la lumière	light
la moyenne	average
le menuisier	carpenter
le serrurier	locksmith

THÉATRE DU CAPITOLE PLEINS FEUX SUR LES COULISSES

Au cœur de la tradition musicale et culturelle de la ville, le théâtre du Capitole participe au rayonnement de Toulouse. Les équipes qui l'animent, autour de Nicolas Joël, directeur artistique, manifestent leur passion à travers la qualité des spectacles offerts. Pour leur part, les services techniques œuvrent dans l'ombre des coulisses. Sans eux, pas de lumière, pas de décors, pas de costumes...Pas de magie.

En moyenne, chaque année, seize spectacles – opéras, opérettes et ballets – sont donnés au théâtre du Capitole, et, généralement, six nouveaux décors sont nécessaires. Menuisiers, serruriers, peintres et sculpteurs les fabriquent ou restaurent la trentaine de décors en stock – le plus ancien, représentant une cour intérieure avec colonnades dans la Grèce ancienne, date de 1947. En professionnels, ils s'adaptent en permanence aux nouvelles techniques et matériaux. Ils travaillent le bois, la résine, le polyester, l'aluminium, etc. De longues heures sont nécessaires pour la fabrication de palais, de villes, de paysages ou d'intérieurs en trompe-l'œil, dont la durée de vie n'excédera pas quinze ans, au mieux. Après: démontage, et récupération ou – hélas – destruction.

a Cherchez dans le texte les mots français qui correspondent à:

dismantling _____

magic _____

teams _____

palaces _____

technical services _____

courtyard _____

wood _____

at the best _____

b Combien de spectacles sont donnés chaque année, en moyenne, au théâtre du Capitole? _____

c Comment s'appelle le directeur artistique du théâtre?

_____

d Combien de décors le théâtre a-t-il en stock? _____

e De quelle année date le plus ancien de ces décors? _____

f En général, pendant combien de temps, au maximum, conserve-t-on les décors? _____

Answers p. 64

A birthday present for Sophie's mother

Sophie	Sandrine, est-ce que tu pourrais pas m'aider pour trouver un cadeau d'anniversaire à ma mère?
Sandrine	Ah, son anniversaire? Mais je sais pas, moi – heum – des bijoux, boucles d'oreille, collier?
Sophie	Ben, disons, l'an dernier, à Noël, je lui ai déjà offert ça.
Sandrine	Je sais pas...des draps – elle n'a pas besoin de draps?
Sophie	Oui, c'est une bonne idée, mais il y a pas quelque chose de plus original?
Sandrine	Oh, plus original, heu, bon, t'as le parfum...
Sophie	Elle est pas très parfum – elle n'aime pas trop ça.
Sandrine	Je sais pas...du papier à lettre?
Sophie	Mais toi, qu'est-ce que tu lui as offert à ta mère, l'an dernier?
Sandrine	Moi, je lui ai offert un peignoir de bain.
Sophie	Ah oui, ça, c'est une bonne idée! Ça te dirait pas d'aller faire les magasins avec moi?
Sandrine	Mais je t'accompagne au magasin où j'ai été, si tu veux.
Sophie	Ah oui, bonne idée!

LISTEN FOR...

un cadeau d'anniversaire	birthday present
des bijoux	jewellery
des draps	sheets
un peignoir de bain	bathrobe

VOCABULARY

la boucle d'oreille	earring
le collier	necklace
avoir besoin de	to need
le parfum	perfume
le papier à lettre	writing paper
offrir	to give
l'idée (f.)	idea

est-ce que tu pourrais pas m'aider ...? would(n't) you be able to help me ...? Like **voudrais** (from the verb **vouloir**), **pourrais** (from **pouvoir**) is an example of the conditional tense (would). You will be getting to grips with it properly in Unit 7.

Ben, disons, l'an dernier, à Noël, je lui ai déjà offert ça Well, you know (literally let's say), last year, at Christmas, I have already given her that (sort of thing).

Elle est pas très parfum – elle n'aime pas trop ça She isn't very into perfume – she isn't too keen on it. The whole of this Conversation is colloquial in style.

Mais toi, qu'est-ce que tu lui as offert à ta mère ...? But what about you – what did you give your mother...? The **lui** is superfluous: Sophie is in effect saying 'What did you give her – your mother, I mean?'

ça te dirait pas d'aller faire les magasins avec moi? you wouldn't like to go and do the shops with me, would you? **Dirait**, like **pourrais**, is from the conditional tense. A present tense example using **dire** in this way: **On va prendre un pot – ça te dit de venir avec nous?** 'We're going for a drink – do you feel like coming with us/what do you say to coming with us/how does that grab you?'

je t'accompagne au magasin où j'ai été I'll take you to the shop I went to (literally I accompany you to the shop where I have been).

7 All of the answers occur in some form in one of the Conversations of this unit. You can ignore accents for crossword purposes.

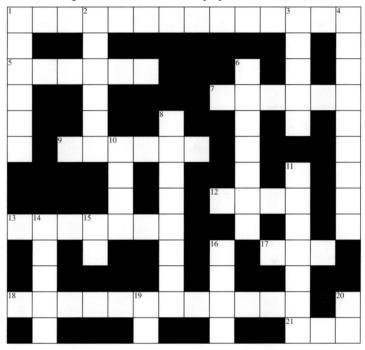

Horizontalement

1. Earring (6,1,7)
5. Garden (6)
7. (Theatre) group (6)
9. Manure (6)
12. Already (4)
13. Shop (7)
17. Been (3)
18. Birthday (12)
21. His/her (sing.) (3)

Verticalement

1. Jewellery (6)
2. Present (6)
3. Premises (5)
4. Outside (9)
6. To find (7)
8. Dressing gown (8)
10. But (4)
11. Parts (7)
14. Beforehand (5)
15. Year (2)
16. Sheet (4)
19. Had (2)
20. We/they (2)

> **Answers p. 64**

Listen to the recording and try to fill in the letter corresponding to the Christmas present which Jean-Pierre decides to buy for:

i.   his mother _____

ii. his father _____

iii. his sister _____

ANSWERS P. 64

iv. Marianne _____

9

Your turn to speak: Marianne is going to visit her friends Francine and Robert and asks you to help her think of a present to take them. As well as the vocabulary from Conversation 3, you will need:

des fleurs	flowers
des chocolats	chocolates
un vase	vase

KEY WORDS
AND PHRASES

le fou	madman
marcher	to walk
s'arrêter	to stop
le jardin	garden
le jardinier	gardener
qu'est-ce que vous faites?	what are you doing?
la scène	stage
l'affiche (f.)	poster
répéter	to repeat, to rehearse
où en es-tu?	where are you at?
où en êtes-vous?	where are you at?
comment ça se passe?	how does it happen?
beaucoup de monde	a lot of people
avez-vous fait la publicité?	have you advertised?
après-demain	the day after tomorrow
le spectacle	show
un cadeau d'anniversaire	birthday present
le bijou, pl. les bijoux	piece of jewellery, pl. jewellery
le drap	sheet
le peignoir de bain	bathrobe
la boucle d'oreille	earring
le collier	necklace
c'est une bonne idée	it's a good idea
quelque chose de plus original	something more original
avoir besoin de	to need
le parfum	perfume
le papier à lettre	writing paper
offrir	to give

GRAMMAR AND EXERCISES

Questions

i.   In informal speech, a sentence is often turned into a yes/no question simply by being said with rising intonation (i.e. the pitch of the voice goes up towards the end). In the Conversations you heard:

Vous avez une salle adaptée?
Vous pensez qu'il va y avoir beaucoup de monde?
Comment vous allez faire?
Elle n'a pas besoin de draps?

ii.   In speech and writing, any statement can be turned into a yes/no question if you put **est-ce que** at the beginning of it:

Est-ce que tu (ne) pourrais pas m'aider pour trouver un cadeau d'anniversaire à ma mère?

iii.   The most elegant way of forming a question is by 'inverting' the main verb and its subject pronoun and putting a hyphen between them. This applies in all tenses:

Pourquoi mettez-vous du fumier sur les fraises?
Où en es-tu avec la troupe de théâtre?
Avez-vous fait la publicité?
Allez-vous bientôt jouer?
Et allez-vous pouvoir répéter avant?

10   Here are some questions in a form in which you might hear them. See if you can rewrite each one in the two forms acceptable in writing: one beginning **Est-ce que**…and the other using inversion. The first one has been done for you.

a   i.   **Tu es là?**

  ii.   *Est-ce que tu es là?*

  iii.   *Es-tu là?*

b   i. **Vous avez froid?**

  ii. _____

  iii. _____

c   i.   **Vous allez jouer bientôt?**

  ii. _____

  iii. _____

d   i.   **Tu vas aux magasins aujourd'hui?**

  ii. _____

  iii. _____

e   i.   **Nous allons à Toulouse?**

  ii. _____

  iii. _____

f   i.   **Il est allemand?**

  ii. _____

  iii. _____

g   i.   **Elle prend des vitamines?**

  ii. _____

  iii. _____

| Answers p. 64 |

More about inversion

There are two tricky bits with this construction. The first comes with **il** and **elle**, where, to ease pronunciation, you have to add an extra **-t-** between the verb and the pronoun if (and only if) the verb ends in a vowel. So:

Il travaille bien.   **Travaille-t-il bien?**
Elle parle français.   **Parle-t-elle français?**
Elle aime le parfum.   **Aime-t-elle le parfum?**
BUT
Il apprend l'italien.   **Apprend-il l'italien?**

(In fact, the '**d**' at the end of **apprend** is pronounced '**t**' in front of a vowel sound such as you have here with **il**. You can hear this on the recording.)

11   Try transforming each of these statements into a question using the construction with inversion. The first one has been done already.

a   Elle habite Paris.

Habite-t-elle Paris?

b   Il travaille chez Renault.

c   Elle apprend l'espagnol.

d   Il a cinquante ans.

e   Il pense à moi.

f   Il fait la cuisine.

g   Elle danse bien.

Answers p. 64

And yet more...

The other complication with inversion comes when the subject is a noun. In that case, the elegant, literary way of forming a question is to put the noun followed by the verb and then the corresponding pronoun:

Le fou parle au jardinier.   **Le fou parle-t-il au jardinier?**
Pierre joue samedi.   **Pierre joue-t-il samedi?**
Anne va voir le spectacle.   **Anne va-t-elle voir le spectacle?**
Sandrine a acheté un peignoir.   **Sandrine a-t-elle acheté un peignoir?**

This construction is sometimes used in speech, but it is rather formal. It would be better for you to stick to the **Est-ce que**… construction for this kind of question.

Responses

Here are some useful phrases for responding to questions:

je pense	I think so
je crois	I believe so
j'espère	I hope so
si possible	if possible
si tout va bien	if all goes well
en principe	in principle
je ne sais pas	I don't know
qui sait?	who knows?
avec plaisir	with pleasure
volontiers	I'd love to
pourquoi pas?	why not?
c'est très gentil, mais...	that's very kind, but...
je suis désolé(e)...	I'm very sorry...
malheureusement...	unfortunately...
je n'ai pas bien compris	I haven't really understood
pouvez-vous répéter?	can you repeat?

12 Can you give a credible answer to each of the following questions, using a different one of those phrases each time? Where there are three dots in the list, you will have to add other words.

There is no one set of right answers, but one possible set is given at the end of the unit.

a Pouvez-vous m'aider, s'il vous plaît?

_____

b Est-ce qu'il va pleuvoir aujourd'hui?

_____

c *Mumble, mumble, mumble.*

_____

d Vous arriverez donc vers six heures?

_____

e Voulez-vous que je vous accompagne?

_____

f Est-ce que cela te dit de venir dîner à la maison?

_____

g C'est Abidjan, la capitale de la Côte d'Ivoire?

_____

Answers p. 64

13 On the recording, Marianne will ask you a series of questions about yourself. You can assume whatever role you like to reply to them. Marianne's questions are on the recording twice: the first time simply with pauses for you to reply and the second time with Jean-Pierre's responses.

14 You have a summer job as a market researcher, working for a company of your choice. See if you can write out ten questions that you might put to interviewees (age, whether they have children, whether they like whisky…). If you are working with a partner, you can take turns at interviewing each other and noting down the responses – which will be more fun if they are not truthful!

_____

_____

_____

_____

_____

_____

_____

_____

_____

_____

EXERCISE 2

3 grapefruit / 1 punnet of blackberries / 1 kilo of grapes / half a kilo of plums / 3 passion-fruit

EXERCISE 4

(a) Paris (b) Andromaque herself (c) Radio
(d) Cassettes (e) Two (f) Thursday and Friday
(g) March

EXERCISE 6

(a) (le) démontage / (la) magie / (les) équipes /
(les) palais / (les) services techniques / (la) cour /
(le) bois / au mieux (b) Seize (c) Nicolas Joël
(d) Une trentaine (e) 1947 (f) Quinze ans

EXERCISE 7

EXERCISE 8

i. b   ii. g   iii. f.   iv. e

EXERCISE 10

(b) ii. Est-ce que vous avez froid? iii. Avez-vous froid? (c) ii. Est-ce que vous allez jouer bientôt? iii. Allez-vous jouer bientôt? (d) ii. Est-ce que tu vas aux magasins aujourd'hui? iii. Vas-tu aux magasins aujourd'hui? (e) ii. Est-ce que nous allons à Toulouse? iii. Allons-nous à Toulouse? (f) ii. Est-ce qu'il est allemand? iii. Est-il allemand? (g) ii. Est-ce qu'elle prend des vitamines? iii. Prend-elle des vitamines?

EXERCISE 11

(b) Travaille-t-il chez Renault? (c) Apprend-elle l'espagnol? (d) A-t-il cinquante ans? (e) Pense-t-il à moi? (f) Fait-il la cuisine? (g) Danse-t-elle bien?

EXERCISE 12

(a) Avec plaisir! (b) Qui sait? (c) Pouvez-vous répéter, s'il vous plaît? Je n'ai pas bien compris. (d) En principe, oui. (e) C'est très gentil, mais j'ai rendez-vous avec un ami (f) Volontiers.
(g) Je crois, oui.

5 HOW THINGS ARE DONE

WHAT YOU WILL LEARN

- ▶ understanding instructions
- ▶ giving instructions to someone you call **vous**
- ▶ giving instructions to someone you call **tu**
- ▶ some first-aid language

Arrête!

POINTS TO REMEMBER

Unit 4 covered the three ways of asking yes/no questions, in particular the 'inversion' method:

Es-tu heureuse?	Are you happy?
Avez-vous compris?	Have you understood?
Allons-nous bientôt partir?	Are we going to leave soon?

BEFORE YOU BEGIN

One of the enjoyable things about starting a new language from scratch is the enormous sense of achievement when you find that native speakers understand you when you say the few words you have mastered. It is ironic that, as you progress in the language, you often get more and more dissatisfied with your efforts: it annoys you when you don't get things absolutely right. If this sounds familiar, it's time to give yourself a talking-to: remind yourself that perfection is an unrealistic expectation. Naturally, a language course will keep telling you the correct way to say things, but that doesn't mean that it is no good at all if you don't get it exactly right. Your measure of success in speaking French at this stage should rather be 'Can French people understand what I am trying to say?'

The first two Conversations of this unit show you how to tell people what to do. The form of the verb used for giving instructions or commands is called the imperative. It is usually the **tu** or **vous** form of the present tense without the **tu** or **vous**:

Viens!	**Venez!**	Come!
Attends!	**Attendez!**	Wait!

How to use the washing machine in the gîte

Christine Vous avez là la machine à laver…

Locataire (tenant) Mm mm…

Christine Vous mettez le linge dans le tambour –
c'est une machine cinq kilos.

Locataire Mm mm.

Christine Vous fermez la porte…fermez…

Locataire Comme ça?

Christine Oui. Voilà. Parfait. Vous fermez la deuxième porte…Appuyez
légèrement…appuyez…voilà. Ici, vous mettez la lessive: là ou il y a le '1', c'est
pour le prélavage, le '2' pour le lavage principal et le '3' pour l'assouplissant.

Locataire Mm mm.

Christine Vous fermez la porte principale: allez-y – appuyez…Parfait!

(Locataire Voilà.)

Christine Vous choisissez le programme sur ce bouton…Choisissez-le…Allez-y…
Tournez-le…

Locataire A gauche?

Christine A gauche…C'est parfait.
Pour démarrer, vous levez ce
bouton: allez-y! Parfait! Très bien!

LISTEN FOR…	
la machine à laver	washing machine
le linge	clothes, linen
appuyez	press
le lavage	wash
ce bouton	this button

c'est une machine cinq kilos it's a five-kilo
machine (i.e. it takes five kilograms of
washing).

le linge clothes. In other contexts, it can also
be translated as 'linen' (e.g. household
linen) or 'underwear'. **Un linge** is 'a
cloth'.

Vous fermez la porte…fermez… You shut
the door… shut (it)… **Vous fermez** is the
straight present tense, followed by the
imperative **fermez**, as Christine tells her
tenant actually to do it.

Vous fermez la deuxième porte You shut the
second door (the first being the door of the
drum).

Ici, vous mettez la lessive Here, you put the
washing powder/liquid; Christine goes on to
explain that the compartment marked '1' is
for the prewash, '2' for the main wash and
'3' for the softener. **La lessive** can also
mean 'washing', e.g. **Je vais faire ma
lessive** 'I'm going to do my washing.'

VOCABULARY	
le tambour	drum
la porte	door
légèrement	lightly
le prélavage	prewash
l'assouplissant (m.)	softener
choisir	to choose
tourner	to turn
démarrer	to start up, to get going
lever	to lift

la porte principale the main door – there are
three doors on this machine!

allez-y! go on! (literally, go to it!).

Choisissez-le… Allez-y… Tournez-le…
Choose it… Go on… Turn it… A pronoun
used with an imperative is tacked on to the
end of it with a hyphen as here. There will
be more about this in the Grammar section.

1

On the recording, the owner of another **gîte** is explaining to a holidaymaker how to use the dishwasher: **le lave-vaisselle**. Listen as many times as you like and see if you can fill in the verbs missing from the transcript below.
La vaisselle here means 'the dirty dishes'; it can also mean 'the washing up'.

Propriétaire	Vous _____ là le lave-vaisselle...
Locataire	Mm mm...
Propriétaire	Vous _____ la vaisselle dans la machine.
Locataire	Mm mm.
Propriétaire	Ici, vous mettez le produit.
Locataire	D'accord.
Propriétaire	Vous _____ la porte: allez-y – _____
Locataire	Voilà.
Propriétaire	Vous _____ le programme sur ce bouton ...
Locataire	Mm mm...
Propriétaire	Le '1', c' _____ pour le prélavage, le '2', c'est pour le lavage normal et le '3' c'est quand il y a très peu de vaisselle. Alors, normalement, on choisit le programme 2... Allez-y...
Locataire	Mm mm...
Propriétaire	_____ le bouton...
Locataire	A gauche?
Propriétaire	Non, à droite... C'est ça. Pour _____ _____, vous appuyez sur ce bouton: _____ Parfait!

Answers p. 80

2

On the recording, Marianne says a series of infinitives with the corresponding imperatives that you would use to someone you called **vous**. Repeating them after her will help you to get the hang of them – and also to practise your pronunciation, particularly of the sounds [i], [é], [r] and the nasal vowel [en].

---

3 See how much of this first-aid advice you can understand:

Dans un accident...
la vie d'un blessé dépend de quelques gestes simples.

Le blessé: saigne-t-il?

- GARDEZ VOTRE SANG-FROID

- EMPECHEZ DES TÉMOINS INCOMPÉTENTS D'EFFECTUER DES MANŒUVRES DANGEREUSES OU INUTILES

- REMUEZ LE BLESSÉ LE MOINS POSSIBLE, MAIS, SI LA SITUATION L'EXIGE, RESPECTEZ L'ALIGNEMENT 'TETE–COU–TRONC'

Si le blessé saigne abondamment

- Allongez-le en respectant l'alignement 'TETE–COU–TRONC'.

- Rassurez-le.

- Découvrez l'endroit qui saigne.

- Appuyez sur la plaie directement avec la main ou mieux avec un linge propre en relâchant de temps en temps (10 minutes).

Si cela continue de couler appuyez encore plus fort.

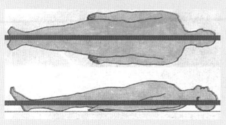

VOCABULARY

le blessé	injured person
empêcher	to prevent
le témoin	witness, bystander
saigner	to bleed
la plaie	wound
relâcher	to let go

Extract from *Codoroute*

a Find in the text the phrases for:

if it continues to flow ⎯⎯⎯⎯⎯⎯⎯⎯⎯⎯⎯⎯⎯⎯⎯

clean cloth ⎯⎯⎯⎯⎯⎯⎯⎯⎯⎯⎯⎯⎯⎯⎯⎯⎯⎯⎯

a few simple actions ⎯⎯⎯⎯⎯⎯⎯⎯⎯⎯⎯⎯⎯⎯

uncover the place which is bleeding ⎯⎯⎯⎯⎯⎯⎯⎯

⎯⎯⎯⎯⎯⎯⎯⎯⎯⎯⎯⎯⎯⎯⎯⎯⎯⎯⎯⎯⎯⎯⎯⎯

keep calm ⎯⎯⎯⎯⎯⎯⎯⎯⎯⎯⎯⎯⎯⎯⎯⎯⎯⎯⎯

move the injured person as little as possible

⎯⎯⎯⎯⎯⎯⎯⎯⎯⎯⎯⎯⎯⎯⎯⎯⎯⎯⎯⎯⎯⎯⎯⎯

b What should you prevent incompetent bystanders from doing?

⎯⎯⎯⎯⎯⎯⎯⎯⎯⎯⎯⎯⎯⎯⎯⎯⎯⎯⎯⎯⎯⎯⎯⎯

c If you haven't got a clean cloth to staunch the wound, what does the text suggest you should use? ⎯⎯⎯⎯⎯⎯⎯⎯⎯⎯⎯⎯⎯

⎯⎯⎯⎯⎯⎯⎯⎯⎯⎯⎯⎯⎯⎯⎯⎯⎯⎯⎯⎯⎯⎯⎯⎯

d If you have to move the injured person, what is the most important rule to observe? ⎯⎯⎯⎯⎯⎯⎯⎯⎯⎯⎯⎯⎯⎯⎯⎯

Answers p. 80

Learning to drive an unfamiliar car

Bruno	Bon. Donc, pour démarrer, voilà – tu as deux clés...donc c'est celle qui a pas de relief...tu la mets dans le...
Stephanie	C'est là?
Bruno	Oui.
Stephanie	Ça tourne pas.
Bruno	Mais pousse!
Stephanie	Non, ça tourne pas.
Bruno	Alors, prends l'autre...
Stephanie	Ça rentre pas.
Bruno	Oh, elle est dans le mauvais sens, alors.
Stephanie	Ça y est!
Bruno	Ça y est. Donc ça s'allume; tu mets au point mort. Tourne la clé...Voilà...Ah! Tu cales! Alors, attends! Avant de démarrer, il faudrait peut-être que tu allumes les lanternes: donc, c'est ce bouton...Voilà, donc, maintenant démarre...Voilà...Donc, tu passes la première; tu as le frein à main là à gauche...voilà...je ferme la porte et tu démarres?...Ah! Il faut...Accélère un peu!

LISTEN FOR...

deux clés	two keys
au point mort	in neutral
les lanternes	sidelights
le frein à main	handbrake

VOCABULARY

pousser	to push
l'autre	the other one
rentrer	to go in
caler	to stall
allumer	to turn on

tu as deux clés...donc c'est celle qui a pas de relief you have two keys...well it's the smooth one (literally the one which doesn't have a raised design). **La clé** can also be spelt **la clef** (as in English on a musical stave).

tu la mets dans le... you put it in the...He can't think of the word.

pousse! push! 'You push' is **tu pousses**, from the verb **pousser**. With **-er** verbs, the final **-s** is dropped to form the **tu** imperative.

elle est dans le mauvais sens it's the wrong way round.

Ça y est! Got it! (literally That there is). Notice the pronunciation.

ça s'allume it's switched on (literally it is lighting itself).

Tourne la clé Turn the key. **Tourner** is an **-er** verb, so the **tu** imperative drops the **-s** from **tu tournes**.

Avant de démarrer Before starting up. Notice the use of the infinitive here and in other such phrases: **avant de partir** 'before leaving', **avant de parler** 'before speaking'.

il faudrait peut-être you should perhaps (literally it would be necessary perhaps). **Il faudrait** is the conditional tense of **il faut** 'it is necessary' and is a very polite alternative to the imperative. A courteous employer will often use it when giving orders to an employee: **Il faudrait ranger ces dossiers** 'These files need putting away'; **Il faudrait faire le repassage** 'The ironing needs doing.'

les lanternes the sidelights. Learn also: **les feux** (m.) 'lights', **les phares** (m.) 'headlights' and **mettre les phares en code** 'to dip headlights/put on the low beams'.

démarre start up. From the verb **démarrer**; being an **-er** verb, it drops the final **-s** of **tu démarres** to form the **tu** imperative.

tu passes la première you go into first (gear). The word for 'gears' is **vitesses** (f.), which literally means 'speeds'.

Accélère un peu! Accelerate a bit! From another **-er** verb: **accélérer**.

PRACTICE

4 You are swapping houses and cars with a French friend for the holiday. On the recording, you teach him to drive your car, reusing a lot of the language from the Conversation. Philippe will prompt you and Marianne will give correct versions of your lines after the pauses.

A driving school

5 On the recording, Philippe teaches his six-year-old daughter Amélie to make instant coffee. The French don't go in for electric kettles, so he has already heated the water and put it in an insulated coffee-jug. You'll need to know the words:

le bouchon	top, stopper
dévisser	to unscrew
verser	to pour
remuer	to stir

You will also hear Philippe saying **Vas-y**! This is the **tu** version of **Allez-y**! 'Go on!' What is odd about it is that the imperative is **Va**! (without the **-s** of **tu vas**), but when it has **-y** tacked on to it, it reacquires the **-s**. There will be more about this in the Grammar section.

a What is the first thing Amélie has to do?

_____

b In what order does Philippe ask her to put the ingredients into the cup?

i. _____

ii. _____

iii. _____

c What is Philippe's final instruction?

Answers p. 80

_____

Amélie

6 Following Philippe's prompts, give instructions to a French visitor on how to use your cordless electric kettle. You are on **tu** terms with the visitor. You'll need the words:

la bouilloire	kettle
la plaque	base (also hotplate)
brancher	to plug in
elle s'arrête automatiquement	it stops automatically

The Lions Club Christmas project

Monique

Je fais partie d'un club…Lions Club – un club de femmes – et, en ce moment, nous avons une activité assez importante, car, pour la période de Noël, nous…récoltons des, des jouets auprès de…de personnes, à la suite d'annonces

faites dans le journal local, pour les distribuer aux familles défavorisées. Nous récupérons les adresses de ces familles auprès des services sociaux de la mairie et, juste avant le jour de Noël, nous apportons dans ces familles ces jouets, pour que les enfants puissent avoir des cadeaux pour Noël. Alors, c'est une activité assez prenante, qui prend beaucoup de temps, parce qu'il faut faire des permanences pour récupérer les jouets, il faut après les trier, ces jouets, parce qu'il y en a qui sont plus ou moins en bon état; après il faut faire les paquets-cadeau, et après aller dans les familles…pauvres de Toulouse, pour distribuer ces paquets. Et, en général, on est accueilli avec beaucoup, beaucoup de plaisir dans ces familles…et on a vraiment l'impression d'être le Père Noël!

VOCABULARY

récolter	to collect (also to harvest)
auprès de	(here) from; also, close to, by
récupérer	obtain
apporter	to take
prenant(e)	absorbing, fascinating
pauvre	poor
le paquet	package, parcel
le plaisir	pleasure

je fais partie d'un club I belong to a club.

nous avons une activité assez importante we're doing quite a lot (literally, we have quite a large activity). **Important** can mean either 'important'(as in English) or 'large' (as here).

la période de Noël the Christmas period. **La période** is not the word for a menstrual period; that is **les règles** (f. and always pl.).

à la suite d'annonces faites dans le journal local following ads placed in the local paper. **Les petites annonces** are the small ads.

pour que les enfants puissent avoir des cadeaux pour Noël so that the children can have presents for Christmas. **Pour que** is

followed by the subjunctive (here **puissent** from the verb **pouvoir**) but, once again, you don't need to use it yourself at this stage.

il faut faire des permanences you have to have someone on duty. The commonest construction with **il faut** is to follow it, as here, with an infinitive. Despite the appearance of the word **permanence**, it does not imply 24 hours a day!

il faut après les trier, ces jouets afterwards, we have to sort them, these toys. The word order here is quite colloquial. A more straightforward form for the sentence would have been **Après, il faut trier ces jouets**. Again, **il faut** is followed by an infinitive.

il y en a qui sont plus ou moins en bon état some of them are in better condition than others (literally there are some of them which are more or less in good condition).

il faut faire les paquets-cadeau you have to gift-wrap them.

on est accueilli you're welcomed (from the verb **accueillir**).

on a vraiment l'impression d'être le Père Noël! you really feel that you're Father Christmas!

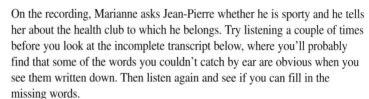

7 On the recording, Jean-Pierre asks you about the Christmas project of Monique and her friends in the Lions Club. The verbs you will need are **récolter**, **donner** and **trier**. All the other words in your part are to be found in Conversation 3.

8 On the recording, Marianne asks Jean-Pierre whether he is sporty and he tells her about the health club to which he belongs. Try listening a couple of times before you look at the incomplete transcript below, where you'll probably find that some of the words you couldn't catch by ear are obvious when you see them written down. Then listen again and see if you can fill in the missing words.

Marianne Tu es sportif, toi?

Jean-Pierre Je ne suis pas vraiment sportif, mais je fais _____ d'un club où

il y a une piscine et un gymnase et j'y vais deux fois par _____

– une fois pour nager et une fois pour faire de la gym.

Marianne Bravo! Et tu connais _____ de gens dans ce club?

Jean-Pierre Un certain nombre, oui, parce qu'en plus nous faisons de temps en temps une

soirée dansante – on le fait à _____, pour la Saint-Valentin,

pour le 14 juillet et puis à la rentrée. Donc là, on peut parler aux gens qu'on

connaît pas, parce qu'on est tous membres du club.

Marianne Ah, c'est _____ s'il y a un côté social aussi.

Jean-Pierre Oui et puis, une fois par an, on fait un effort humanitaire: nous récoltons des

vêtements en bon _____ pour les envoyer dans des pays

_____

Marianne Tu en veux en ce _____ , des vêtements?

Jean-Pierre Oui.

Marianne Alors je vais t'en donner: j'ai des pulls qui sont trop petits pour moi, des

_____ que je ne mets plus et puis un manteau qui n'est plus à

la mode mais qui tient chaud.

Jean-Pierre Ah ben très bien! Merci!

Answers p. 80

9 Back to some of the dos and don'ts of first aid:

SECOURIR

— Il ne faut jamais donner à manger ou à boire à un blessé, même pas de l'eau et surtout pas d'alcool.

— Il ne faut pas déplacer un blessé ou tenter de l'extraire du véhicule, sauf, bien sûr, en cas d'incendie.

— Il faut couvrir un blessé avec une couverture ou un vêtement, surtout s'il pleut. Un blessé a toujours froid.

— Il faut réconforter les blessés qui n'ont pas perdu connaissance ainsi que les autres personnes non blessées mais bouleversées par l'accident.

— Il ne faut jamais:
  • ÉVACUER UN BLESSÉ SANS ATTENDRE LES SECOURS
  • ABANDONNER UN BLESSÉ APPAREMMENT MORT

Extract from *Codoroute*

VOCABULARY	
secourir/les secours	to help/help
l'incendie (m.)	fire

Which of the following is TRUE and which FALSE?

TRUE / FALSE

a The first thing you should do after an accident is to pull any injured people out of their cars. ☐ ☐

b You should drive anyone seriously injured to hospital rather than waiting for an ambulance to arrive. ☐ ☐

c You should try to comfort not only the injured but anyone who is in shock from the accident. ☐ ☐

d You should keep the injured as cool as possible. ☐ ☐

e You should give them a cup of sweet tea. ☐ ☐

f You shouldn't leave them, even if they appear to be dead. ☐ ☐

Answers p. 80

la machine à laver	washing machine
la lessive	washing/washing powder/liquid
je vais faire ma lessive	I'm going to do my washing
le linge	clothes
appuyer	to press
légèrement	lightly
le bouton	button
la porte	door
choisir	to choose
tourner	to turn
démarrer	to start up, to get going
lever	to lift
allez-y!	go on!
la clé	key
l'autre	the other one
rentrer	to go in
au point mort	in neutral
les feux (m.)	lights
les lanternes	sidelights
les phares (m.)	headlights
mettre les phares en code	to dip headlights
le frein à main	handbrake
pousser	to push
caler	to stall
ça y est!	got it! done it!
tu passes la première	you go into first (gear)
les vitesses (f.)	gears (literally speeds)
accélérer	to accelerate
des jouets	toys
défavorisés	underprivileged
les services sociaux	social services
trier	to sort
le paquet	package, parcel
important(e)	large
je fais partie d'un club	I belong to a club
l'annonce (f.)	ad
le journal local	local paper
il faut faire des permanences	you have to have someone on duty
récolter	to harvest, to collect
la récolte	harvest
récupérer	obtain
apporter	to bring
distribuer	to distribute
les familles pauvres	poor families
plus ou moins	more or less
en bon état	in good condition
les paquets-cadeau	gift-wrapped parcels
le plaisir	pleasure
le Père Noël	Father Christmas

GRAMMAR AND EXERCISES

The imperative (command form)

Vous

For most verbs the imperative used to someone called **vous** is exactly the same as the **vous** form of the present tense, minus the word **vous**:

travailler	vous travaillez	travaillez!	work!
finir	vous finissez	finissez!	finish!
dire	vous dites	dites!	say!

Tu

For most verbs, the imperative used to someone called **tu** is the same as the **tu** form of the present tense, but without the word **tu**:

revenir	tu reviens	reviens!	come back!
dormir	tu dors	dors!	sleep!
sourire	tu souris	souris!	smile!

In verbs which have an infinitive ending in **-er**, the **-s** at the end of the **tu** form disappears in the imperative:

rester	tu restes	reste!	stay!
écouter	tu écoutes	écoute!	listen!
marcher	tu marches	marche!	walk!

10 See if you can complete the table with the **tu** and the **vous** forms of the imperative of the verbs shown:

Infinitive	Tu imperative	Vous imperative
venir	viens!	venez!
tenir	_____	_____
parler	_____	_____
dire	_____	_____
apprendre	_____	_____
aller	_____	_____
finir	_____	_____
choisir	_____	_____
tourner	_____	_____

Answers p. 80

Nous

There is one other form known as an imperative. It corresponds to 'Let's…' in English:

allons! let's go!
voyons! let's see!
partons! let's be off!
mangeons! let's eat!

As you see, it is simply the **nous** form of the verb without the **nous**.

Irregulars

As ever, there are a few – but very few – irregular forms:

être	sois!	soyons!	soyez!
avoir	aie!	ayons!	ayez!
savoir	sache!	sachons!	sachez!

You can hear those words pronounced on the recording.

Sois sage!	Be good!
Soyez gentils!	Be kind!
Ayons un peu de courage!	Let's have a bit of courage!
Ayez pitié!	Have pity!
Sache la vérité!	Know the truth!
Sachez que je suis avec vous!	Know that I am with you!

11 How would you say the following in French?

a Let's go to the beach! _____

b Let's drink champagne! _____

c Let's take the car! _____

d Children! Be good! **Les** _____

e Let's learn Italian! _____

f Know (**tu**) that I love you! _____

g Have (**vous**) a bit of courage! _____

_____

Answers p. 80

The imperative with a pronoun

An object pronoun (e.g. him, them, to it, of it) combines with an imperative by being tacked on to the end of it with a hyphen:

allez-y!	go to it!
écoutez-moi!	listen to me!
parlez-lui!	talk to him/her!
prends-en!	take some!
apprends-le! (e.g. **le français**)	learn it!
vends-la! (e.g. **la voiture**)	sell it!

With **-er** verbs, if **-y** or **-en** is tacked on to the end of a **tu** form imperative, the **-s** reappears to separate the two vowels:

aller	**tu vas**	**va!/vas-y!**	go!/go to it!
penser	**tu penses**	**pense!/penses-y!**	think!/think about it!
parler	**tu parles**	**parle!/parles-en!**	talk!/talk about it!
manger	**tu manges**	**mange!/manges-en!**	eat!/eat some!

12 Looking at the models above, work out how to say:

a Understand me! (**tu**) _____

b Think about it! (**vous**) _____

c Sell them! (**vous**) _____

d Listen to us! (**tu**) _____

e Eat some! (**vous**) _____

f Let's talk about it! _____

Answers p. 80

The imperative of reflexive verbs

Reflexive verbs follow the pattern of the imperative with a pronoun. Note that **te** changes to **toi**.

se lever 'to get up':
| **lève-toi!** | **levons-nous!** | **levez-vous!** |

s'asseoir 'to sit down':
| **assieds-toi!** | **asseyons-nous!** | **asseyez-vous!** |

se dépêcher 'to hurry':
| **dépêche-toi!** | **dépêchons-nous!** | **dépêchez-vous!** |

se débrouiller 'to cope, to get by, to sort things out on your own':
| **débrouille-toi!** | **débrouillons-nous!** | **débrouillez-vous!** |

13 What are the three imperative forms of the verbs below?

	tu	nous	vous
se reposer	_____	_____	_____
se coucher	_____	_____	_____
s'amuser	_____	_____	_____

Answers p. 80

14 To consolidate what you have learned, write out a dozen or so commands, some using the **tu** form of the imperative and some the **vous** form. If you are working with a partner, take turns to issue your commands to each other – and to mime obeying them!

15 On the recording, Marianne gives instructions for getting into the centre of the maze – **le labyrinthe**. See if you can follow them!

↑ vous êtes ici

When you have done that successfully, you'll find it helpful to go through it again, this time marking the correct route on the maze. Then try giving the instructions yourself. If you are working with a partner, one of you can give the instructions for getting into the centre and the other the instructions for finding the way out again.

EXERCISE 1

avez / mettez / fermez / appuyez / choisissez / est / Tournez / démarrer / allez-y

EXERCISE 3

(a) si cela continue de couler / un linge propre / quelques gestes simples / découvrez l'endroit qui saigne / gardez votre sang-froid / remuez le blessé le moins possible (b) carrying out dangerous or useless manœuvres (c) your hand (d) maintaining the alignment of head, neck and trunk

EXERCISE 5

(a) Turn/unscrew the top of the coffee-jug.
(b) i. Hot water ii. Coffee iii. One sugar (c) Stir!

EXERCISE 8

partie / semaine / beaucoup / Noël / agréable / état / pauvres / moment / jupes

EXERCISE 9

(a) False (b) False (c) True (d) False (e) False
(f) True

EXERCISE 10

tiens! tenez! / parle! parlez! / dis! dites! / apprends! apprenez! / va! allez! / finis! finissez! / choisis! choisissez! / tourne! tournez!

EXERCISE 11

(a) Allons à la plage! (b) Buvons du champagne!
(c) Prenons la voiture/l'auto! (d) Les enfants! Soyez sages! (e) Apprenons l'italien! (f) Sache que je t'aime! (g) Ayez un peu de courage!

EXERCISE 12

(a) Comprends-moi! (b) Pensez-y!
(c) Vendez-les! (d) Écoute-nous! (e) Mangez-en!
(f) Parlons-en!

EXERCISE 13

repose-toi! reposons-nous! reposez-vous!
couche-toi! couchons-nous! couchez-vous!
amuse-toi! amusons-nous! amusez-vous!

WHAT YOU WILL LEARN

▶ understanding what people say about the future
▶ talking about the future yourself
▶ making arrangements to meet

POINTS TO REMEMBER

One way of talking about things which are going to happen is by using the verb **aller** followed by an infinitive:

Je vais parler à mon chef	I'm going to speak to my boss
Il va m'écouter	He's going to listen to me

In English you can say either 'He is going to listen' or 'He will listen'. In the same way, French has two ways of talking about the future and most of the time you can use either of them. In this unit, you will meet the one that is equivalent to 'He will listen'.

BEFORE YOU BEGIN

A favourite expression of language teachers is **le bain linguistique**, literally, 'the linguistic bath'. An easy way of achieving it at home or in the car is with cassettes or French broadcasts. Soaking in the language like this relaxes you (like a bubble bath!) so that you don't panic the moment you hear a stream of French. Even if you are not paying a great deal of attention, it gives you practice at picking out the words you know from all those you don't. And (again like the best bubble baths) it softens you up to be receptive in your more active forms of language learning.

Arranging to meet for lunch

LISTEN FOR...

je serai	I shall be
disponible	available, free
je t'attendrai	I'll wait for you

Séverine	Allo?
Sophie	Allo, Séverine – c'est Sophie à l'appareil. Ça va?
Séverine	Ça va – et toi?
Sophie	Oui, oui, ça va. Je t'appelais parce que demain je serai en ville – j'ai un cours demain matin – et je serai disponible à midi et demi. Ça te dirait de manger avec moi?
Séverine	Oui – c'est une bonne idée. Midi et demi? Oui, oui, oui, c'est bon pour moi.
Sophie	Alors, je t'attendrai devant la poste, midi et demi, une heure moins le quart. Ça va?
Séverine	Très bien. Je serai là...à midi et demi.
Sophie	D'accord. Alors, à demain!
Séverine	D'accord. Je t'embrasse. Au revoir!
Sophie	Bye!

c'est Sophie à l'appareil it's Sophie (on the phone) – standard telephone-speak.

Ça va? / Ça va Are you all right? / Yes, I'm all right.

Je t'appelais parce que demain je serai en ville I was calling you because tomorrow I shall be in town. **Je serai** 'I shall be' is from the future tense of the verb **être**. 'You will be' is **tu seras**: **Seras-tu disponible?** 'Will you be available?' There will be more explanation in the Grammar section.

j'ai un cours I have a class.

Ça te dirait de manger avec moi? Would you fancy eating with me? (literally That to you would say to eat with me?) **Dirait** is from

the conditional (would) tense, which will be covered in Unit 7. For now, learn the present tense versions: **Ça te dit? / Ça vous dit?** 'Do you fancy that?'

Je t'attendrai devant la poste I'll wait for you in front of the post office. **J'attendrai** is from the future of the verb **attendre**. 'You will wait for' is **tu attendras**: **Tu m'attendras? – Oui! Je t'attendrai!**

Ça va? (here) Is that OK?

Je t'embrasse literally I kiss you. Friends often end a phone call or a letter like this. An English equivalent would be 'lots of love'.

Bye! The English word – the Italian 'ciao!' is also often used.

1

On the recording, Marianne rings Jean-Pierre to say that she will be making a business trip to Aix-en-Provence, where he lives. Listen to their conversation and see if you can catch the information below:

a On which day will Marianne be going to Aix?

_____

b At what time is her business appointment?

_____

c Will Jean-Pierre be at home on Friday morning?

_____

d Where do Marianne and Jean-Pierre arrange to meet?

_____

e At what time do they arrange to meet?

Answers p. 96

_____

Aix-en-Provence

2

You ring Marianne and arrange to have dinner with her. When you have to make a phone-call in a foreign language, it is a good idea to prepare in advance some of the things you are likely to want to say. For this call, you'll be needing

Ça va?   **Écoute!**
Je serai à Paris ce week-end.   **Seras-tu disponible samedi soir?**
Parfait!   **A samedi!**

Philippe will guide you.

3 Here is a letter from Patrice to his friend Jean-Luc in Toulouse:

Lyon

le 22 mars

Cher Jean-Luc,

J'espère que tu vas bien – et que tu n'es pas parti en vacances en ce moment. J'ai essayé quatre ou cinq fois de te téléphoner, mais tu n'étais pas là. Moi, je pars ce soir: j'ai des rendez-vous de travail à Aix, à Marseille, à Montpellier et... jeudi prochain, à Toulouse! Je travaillerai toute la journée, mais je serai libre vers six heures du soir. Seras-tu disponible? Malheureusement, je dois rentrer le soir même – mon train part à 20h03 - mais, si tu es libre, on pourra au moins prendre un pot ensemble. Je vais essayer de nouveau de te téléphoner, mais, si jamais je n'arrive pas à te contacter, je t'attendrai de 18h à 18h30 au Bar des Anglais.
Bien à toi,

Patrice

a Why is Patrice going to Toulouse?

_____

b Why is he writing rather than making arrangements by telephone?

_____

c Will he be spending Thursday night in Toulouse?

_____

d Where does he say he will wait for Jean-Luc?

_____

e Between what times will he be there?

_____

f Can you find in the text the French for the following?

my train leaves at… _____

to have a drink together _____

Answers p. 96

I hope you are well _____

Unmanned exploration of Mars

Intervieweuse

Quels types d'explorations sont envisagés avant d'envoyer des hommes sur Mars?

M. Vaillant

Alors, il y a plusieurs expériences qui sont prévues dans le futur. Une première expérience assez astucieuse consiste à envoyer un engin suspendu à un ballon qui sera largué sur Mars. Alors, l'avantage de ce système, est que, lorsqu'il fait chaud, lorsque le jour se lève sur Mars, le soleil réchauffera le ballon et, donc, le ballon montera. Et sur Mars, il y a du vent, donc le vent poussera le ballon, donc il se déplacera sans consommer d'énergie et, quand la nuit tombera, le, le ballon tombera, et donc le, l'engin sera à un autre endroit sur le sol de Mars et pourra faire des expériences. Et, en même temps, il y aura un satellite qui tournera autour de Mars et qui permettra de recueillir des informations. Donc ça, cette expérience permettra de connaître un certain nombre d'informations sur le sol de Mars, sur la température, sur les vents, etc.

LISTEN FOR...

plusieurs expériences	several experiments
un engin	a machine
un ballon	a balloon
réchauffera	will heat up

VOCABULARY

envisager	to envisage
envoyer	to send
prévoir (past part. **prévu(es)**)	to plan, to foresee
astucieux, -euse	clever
suspendre (past part. **suspendu**)	to suspend
se déplacer	to move

avant d'envoyer before sending. Notice the two other phrases in this Conversation which use an infinitive where English uses a form in -ing:

consiste à envoyer
consists in sending

sans consommer d'énergie
without consuming any energy

qui sera largué which will be dropped/let loose. You have already met **je serai** and **tu seras**; **il sera** and **elle sera** are also from the future tense of **être**.

lorsque le jour se lève when day rises. **Lorsque** is another word for **quand**, 'when'.

réchauffera...montera...poussera... se déplacera...tombera... tournera... will heat up...will rise...will push...will move...will fall...will turn. All are **il/elle** forms of the future tense following the same regular pattern (the infinitive with **-a** on the end). More on this in the Grammar section.

sera à un autre endroit sur le sol de Mars will be in another place on the surface of Mars. **Le sol** also means 'ground' or 'soil'.

pourra faire des expériences will be able to make experiments. **Une expérience** can be either an experiment or an experience. **Pourra** is from the future tense of the verb **pouvoir** 'to be able'.

il y aura there will be – the future of **il y a**.

qui permettra de recueillir des informations which will make it possible to gather information. Notice the plural form of **informations**.

4 Looking once again at the transcript of Conversation 2, see if you can underline the thirteen verbs in the future tense.

Answers p. 96

5 An information leaflet gives the following account of the type of exploration Monsieur Vaillant described in the Conversation:

Le Mars Balloon Relay est embarqué à bord d'un satellite d'exploration et d'observation de Mars. Ce satellite utilisera un certain nombre d'instruments pour mener pendant 688 jours, soit une année martienne, des études sur le sol et le sous-sol martien, l'atmosphère et le champ magnétique. La durée de ces études couvrira un cycle complet et fournira une cartographie extrêmement précise de Mars.

Le Mars Balloon Relay est un ensemble émetteur-récepteur-antenne dont la mission consiste à collecter les données d'expériences

MISE A POSTE DE L'AEROSTAT

scientifiques réalisées sur le sol de la planète rouge par différentes sondes d'explorations. Ces données seront alors retransmises en direction de la Terre pour leur traitement. ■

See if you can find the following phrases in the text:

the red planet ———————————————————————

a Martian year ———————————————————————

transmitter-receiver ———————————————————————

the Earth ———————————————————————

the magnetic field ———————————————————————

processing (literally treatment) ———————————————————————

a mapping ———————————————————————

Answers p. 96   the data from scientific experiments ———————————————————————

6 On the recording is a description of two clever ideas for generating electricity. What are they? Don't worry about the words you don't understand – just try to catch enough of the gist to tell what Marianne and Jean-Pierre are talking about.

Answers p. 96

7 Your friend Paul will soon be starting a new job (**Il sera technicien**). Jean-Pierre asks you about it on the recording. You'll need the future tenses: **il commencera**, **il sera**, **il fera** (from **faire**), **il travaillera** and **il prendra**.

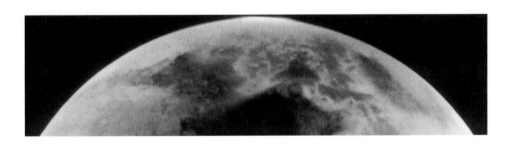

A coach tour of the Midi-Pyrénées region

Guide

Eh bien, nous commencerons notre découverte de la région Midi-Pyrénées par un arrêt dans un village qui s'appelle Lisle-sur-Tarn, qui se trouve à l'est de Toulouse. Nous effectuerons dans la journée un périple d'une centaine de kilomètres. Vous pourrez ainsi découvrir une capitale, Albi, avec une cathédrale que vous admirerez, avec ses peintures, avec ses sculptures…Vous pourrez également découvrir le musée d'Henri de Toulouse-Lautrec et ainsi, nous avons là un des exemples les plus célèbres de notre patrimoine régional. Nous accompagnerons cette découverte par la visite du village de Cordes: Cordes, un des villages les plus pittoresques de France, une bastide construite au moyen âge, et qui marque la mémoire de nos comtes de Toulouse.

> ## LISTEN FOR...
>
> Proper names:
> **Lisle-sur-Tarn**
> **Albi**
> **Henri de Toulouse-Lautrec**
> **Cordes**

VOCABULARY

la découverte, découvrir	discovery, to discover
l'arrêt (m.)	stop
l'est (m.)	east
ainsi	thus
la peinture	painting
célèbre	famous
le patrimoine	heritage
la bastide	walled town (also Provençal farmhouse)

nous commencerons we shall start. The **nous** form of the future ends in **-ons**. As you have seen already, the beginning of the word is usually the infinitive.

Nous effectuerons dans la journée un périple d'une centaine de kilomètres We shall, in the course of the day, complete a tour of about a hundred kilometres. The style of the guide's speech is quite formal. A more informal way of saying the same thing would be to use the future of the verb **faire** (**nous ferons**) and **un circuit** rather than **un périple**: **Nous ferons un circuit d'une centaine de kilomètres dans la journée**. You could also say simply **Nous ferons une centaine de kilomètres dans la journée**.

Vous pourrez You will be able. You have already met **pourra**, from the future of **pouvoir**. The **vous** form of the future ends in **-ez**.

une capitale, Albi Albi was the capital of its own little kingdom until the tenth century, when it joined forces with Toulouse. Albi is known as **la ville rouge**, because it is built of red brick, and Toulouse is called **la ville rose**, because it is built of rather pinker brick! And yet it is in Toulouse that probes are being constructed to be sent to **la planète rouge**!

vous admirerez you will admire. Quite a tongue-twister! Again, the **vous** form of the future ends in **-ez**. The first part of the word is most often the infinitive.

un des villages les plus pittoresques de France one of the most picturesque villages in France. Further examples of this construction: **le village le plus pittoresque de la région** 'the most picturesque village in the region'; **la ville la plus intéressante de la région** 'the most interesting town in the region'.

qui marque la mémoire de nos comtes de Toulouse which recalls our counts of Toulouse (literally which marks the memory of).

8

You are going to a reception for a party from your twin town or village in France. The organiser of the next day's coach outing asks you to act as interpreter so that he can tell the visitors about it. Here's the text of what he is going to say. Look back to Conversation 3 to help you prepare, then turn on the recording and see if you can cope!

Tomorrow we shall visit the region.

We shall do about a hundred kilometres in the day.

We shall start with the visit of a little village...

it's the most picturesque village in the region.

You will be able to discover the principal town of the region.

I am sure you will like the cathedral...

and you will admire the paintings of the museum.

And then, in the afternoon, we shall visit a school...

and you will be able to speak French to the children.

9 On the recording, Frédéric asks Jacqueline about her holiday plans. In her reply, she uses the curious French construction:

Nous avons l'intention, avec Roger, de partir pour le Maroc.

Contrary to the logic of the structure, this does not imply that there will be anyone other than Roger and Jacqueline in the party. It would translate: We (that's Roger and I) are intending to go off to Morocco.

You have now met all but one of the endings of the future tense. The remaining one is the **ils/elles** form, which ends in **-ont**. You will hear two examples of it in this recording: **recevront** (from the future of **recevoir**, 'to receive' or 'give hospitality to someone') and **feront** (from the future of **faire**).

a Will Jacqueline and Roger be flying to Marrakesh?

_____

b Have they already booked a hire-car?

_____

c Have they already worked out a precise itinerary?

_____

d Whose address have they been given?

_____

e. How long will Jacqueline and Roger stay with them?

_____

f What will these people do for them?

_____

g In which direction will they head after that?

_____

h What do they intend to do there?

_____

Here is the transcript of the recording to help you:

Frédéric   Jacqueline, quels sont tes projets de voyage pour les mois qui viennent?

Jacqueline   Pour les mois qui viennent, nous avons l'intention, avec Roger, de partir pour le Maroc.

Frédéric   Et vous y partirez en voiture?

Jacqueline   Non! Nous prendrons l'avion jusqu'à Marrakech, et là, nous louerons une voiture.

Frédéric   Vous l'avez déjà réservée?

Jacqueline   Nous l'avons réservée, bien sûr, et nous partirons sans avoir d'itinéraire précis – nous verrons sur place. De toute façon, nous avons l'intention d'aller chez des Berbères dont on nous a donné l'adresse; ils nous recevront pendant trois jours, ils nous feront visiter leur région, et ensuite nous partirons un peu plus dans le sud où, là aussi, nous avons l'intention de retrouver des…des habitants du pays pour nous faire visiter également leur région.

Answers p. 96

KEY WORDS AND PHRASES

c'est Sophie à l'appareil	it's Sophie (on the phone)
ça va? / Ça va	Are you all right? / I'm all right
je serai disponible	I shall be available, free
je t'attendrai	I'll wait for you
j'ai un cours	I have a class
ça te dit? / ça vous dit?	do you fancy that?
je t'embrasse	lots of love (literally I kiss you)
envisager	to envisage
prévoir (past part. prévu)	to plan, to foresee
avant d'envoyer	before sending
astucieux, -euse	clever
suspendre (past part. suspendu)	to suspend
lorsque le jour se lève	when day rises
le ballon se déplacera	the balloon will move
à un autre endroit	in another place
l'engin (m.) pourra faire des expériences	the machine will be able to make experiments
il y aura	there will be – the future of il y a
la découverte	discovery
l'arrêt (m.)	stop
l'est (m.)	east
ainsi	thus
la peinture	painting
célèbre	famous
le patrimoine	heritage
la bastide	walled town (also Provençal farmhouse)
le village le plus pittoresque de la région	the most picturesque village in the region

GRAMMAR AND EXERCISES

The future tense

The endings of the future tense are <u>always</u> regular – even for the verb **être**! They are: **-ai**, **-as**, **-a**, **-a**, **-ons**, **-ez**, **-ont**, **-ont** – the same as the endings of the present tense of **avoir**. With most verbs, these endings are put on the end of the infinitive:

j'habiter<u>ai</u>	nous habiter<u>ons</u>	je finir<u>ai</u>	nous finir<u>ons</u>
tu habiter<u>as</u>	vous habiter<u>ez</u>	tu finir<u>as</u>	vous finir<u>ez</u>
il habiter<u>a</u>	ils habiter<u>ont</u>	il finir<u>a</u>	ils finir<u>ont</u>
elle habiter<u>a</u>	elles habiter<u>ont</u>	elle finir<u>a</u>	elles finir<u>ont</u>

When the infinitive ends in **-re**, the final **-e** is dropped:

j'attendrai	nous attendrons
tu attendras	vous attendrez
il attendra	ils attendront
elle attendra	elles attendront

Similarly, the future tense of **vendre** is **je vendrai**, etc. and **prendre** gives **je prendrai**, etc.

10 To help you get the hang of the basic forms, write alongside each of these infinitives the part of the future tense which is indicated:

travailler   ils _____

descendre   elle _____

monter   tu _____

vivre   vous _____

servir   je _____

pousser   nous _____

démarrer   il _____

repartir   elles _____

Answers p. 96

11 See if you can fill in the future-tense verbs in this extract from a letter written by a teacher who is hosting a school visit from abroad. The infinitives are given in brackets.

Vos élèves [coucher] _____chez les enfants de ma classe et [prendre]

_____le petit déjeuner et le repas du soir en famille. Pendant la

journée, ils [être] _____à l'école avec leurs correspondants français et

ils [déjeuner] _____ensemble à la cantine. Le mercredi après-midi,

nous [partir] _____au bord de la mer et le samedi après-midi nous

[permettre] _____aux enfants de visiter la ville et de faire des courses

en compagnie de leurs correspondants.

Answers p. 96

Irregular future stems

Although the endings are always regular in the future tense, there are a few verbs for which the beginning (the 'stem') is irregular. The main ones are:

être

je serai	nous serons
tu seras	vous serez
il sera	ils seront
elle sera	elles seront

avoir

j'aurai	nous aurons
tu auras	vous aurez
il aura	ils auront
elle aura	elles auront

aller

j'irai	nous irons
tu iras	vous irez
il ira	ils iront
elle ira	elles iront

savoir

je saurai	nous saurons
tu sauras	vous saurez
il saura	ils sauront
elle saura	elles sauront

pouvoir

je pourrai	nous pourrons
tu pourras	vous pourrez
il pourra	ils pourront
elle pourra	elles pourront

devoir

je devrai	nous devrons
tu devras	vous devrez
il devra	ils devront
elle devra	elles devront

tenir (and its compounds)

je tiendrai	nous tiendrons
tu tiendras	vous tiendrez
il tiendra	ils tiendront
elle tiendra	elles tiendront

venir (and its compounds)

je viendrai	nous viendrons
tu viendras	vous viendrez
il viendra	ils viendront
elle viendra	elles viendront

voir

je verrai	nous verrons
tu verras	vous verrez
il verra	ils verront
elle verra	elles verront

envoyer

j'enverrai	nous enverrons
tu enverras	vous enverrez
il enverra	ils enverront
elle enverra	elles enverront

falloir (il faut): il faudra

pleuvoir (il pleut): il pleuvra

12 Write a bad-tempered reply to each of the commands below, on the model:

- **Envoie-moi ta photo!**
- **Non! Je ne t'enverrai pas ma photo!**

a – Prends la première rue à gauche!

– Non! _____

b – Tiens Thierry par la main!

– Non! _____

c – Apprends l'espagnol!

– Non! _____

d – Reviens vite!

– Non! _____

e – Va voir ta grand-mère!

– Non! _____

e – Viens avec moi!

– Non! _____

g – Envoie ton curriculum vitae au directeur!

– Non! _____

Answers p. 96

13 See if you can complete each of the sentences below with the correct form of the future tense for each of the verbs shown.

a Nous _____là avec toi. [être]

b Ils _____vers huit heures. [venir]

c Demande à Jeanne-Marie: elle _____. [savoir]

d Je ne _____pas venir. [pouvoir]

e Il _____y aller à pied. [falloir]

f Est-ce que vous _____au musée? [aller]

g Tu m' _____une carte postale? [envoyer]

h Demain, c'est l'anniversaire de Jean: il _____vingt-huit ans. [avoir]

Answers p. 96

AND FINALLY...

14 On the recording, you will hear a man called Jean-Marie on the phone arranging to have lunch with his friend and colleague Maryvonne. Her diary for the week is shown below. Listen and write in the appointment she makes with Jean-Marie. Then, if you're working with someone else, have a go at roleplaying the same kind of telephone call. One of you initiates the call and suggests lunch and the other takes over Maryvonne's diary (including the date with Jean-Marie). Be sure to fix where and when you are meeting. If you're learning on your own, try playing both parties to the conversation – and do work aloud to give yourself practice at getting your tongue round the words.

Answers p. 96

MAI

lundi 18
10h – 15h Session de travail chez France-Imper

mardi 19
9h – 18h Chez Philibert

mercredi 20
12h30 Déjeuner avec M. Alambert

jeudi 21
16h Mme. Masson

vendredi 22
9h – 11h Réunion du Comité RD

15 What are your plans for the next twelve months? The most useful verbs for expressing them are likely to be:

Je ferai / Nous ferons
Je serai / Nous serons
J'aurai / Nous aurons
J'irai/ Nous irons
Je prendrai / Nous prendrons
J'attendrai / Nous attendrons
Je changerai / Nous changerons
Je resterai / Nous resterons

See if you can write ten sentences about what you will do. Then tell your partner (if you have one) all about it. Jean-Pierre's answer to this exercise is given on the recording.

EXERCISE 1

(a) Friday   (b) 10 a.m.   (c) No   (d) In front of his house   (e) 12.30

EXERCISE 3

(a) For a business meeting   (b) He has tried four or five times to phone but Jean-Luc was not there
(c) No (he has to go home that evening)   (d) At the Bar des Anglais   (e) 6 – 6.30 p.m.   (f) Mon train part à… / Prendre un pot ensemble / J'espère que tu vas bien.

EXERCISE 4

sera (largué) / réchauffera / montera / poussera / (se) déplacera / tombera / tombera / sera / pourra / (il y) aura / tournera / permettra / permettra

EXERCISE 5

la planète rouge / une année martienne / émetteur-récepteur / la Terre / le champ magnétique / (le) traitement / une cartographie / les données d'expériences scientifiques

EXERCISE 6

Generating electricity (a) through solar energy panels and (b) through wind-power.
Les panneaux are 'panels', le toit means 'the roof', le moulin à vent is 'the windmill' and les ailes are 'the sails' (literally wings). Here is what Jean-Pierre and Marianne said:

Jean-Pierre

Il y a un système astucieux pour avoir de l'electricité pas cher. Ça consiste à mettre des panneaux spéciaux sur le toit de la maison. Pendant la journée, le soleil les réchauffe. Les panneaux conservent l'énergie solaire et la transforment en électricité. Alors, ça permet de faire marcher la lumière, le chauffage, etc. sans payer l'électricité.

Marianne

Un autre système également astucieux consiste à installer des moulins à vent. En général, on ne le fait pas pour une seule maison – on le fait sur la surface de la mer, par exemple. Donc, le vent souffle et il fait tourner les ailes des moulins. Et puis il y a un engin qui transforme le mouvement des ailes en électricité.

EXERCISE 9

(a) Yes   (b) Yes   (c) No   (d) That of some Berbers
(e) 3 days   (f) Give them hospitality and take them round their region   (g) South   (h) Find some local people to show them round that region

EXERCISE 10

ils travailleront / elle descendra / tu monteras / vous vivrez / je servirai / nous pousserons / il démarrera / elles repartiront

EXERCISE 11

coucheront / prendront / seront / déjeuneront / partirons / permettrons

EXERCISE 12

(a) Non! Je ne prendrai pas la première rue à gauche!   (b) Non! Je ne tiendrai pas Thierry par la main!   (c) Non! Je n'apprendrai pas l'espagnol!
(d) Non! Je ne reviendrai pas vite!   (e) Non! Je n'irai pas voir ma grand-mère!   (f) Non! Je ne viendrai pas avec toi!   (g) Non! Je n'enverrai pas mon curriculum vitae au directeur!

EXERCISE 13

(a) serons   (b) viendront   (c) saura   (d) pourrai
(e) faudra   (f) irez   (g) enverras   (h) aura

EXERCISE 14

Vendredi 22: 12h, au Restaurant des Comtes de Toulouse

7

WHAT IF...?

WHAT YOU
WILL LEARN

WHAT YOU
WILL LEARN
- ▶ how to say what <u>will</u> happen if…
- ▶ how to say what <u>would</u> happen if…

POINTS TO
REMEMBER

Can you remember how the future tense of **parler** goes?

je parlerai	**nous parlerons**
tu parleras	**vous parlerez**
il parlera	**ils parleront**
elle parlera	**elles parleront**

What about the imperfect tense?

je parlais	**nous parlions**
tu parlais	**vous parliez**
il parlait	**ils parlaient**
elle parlait	**elles parlaient**

If you have forgotten the imperfect, you can refresh your memory by looking back at Unit 3.

BEFORE YOU
BEGIN

This unit will introduce the conditional tense, which corresponds to the English 'would': 'they would work', 'he would like', 'you would go', etc. Its forms are hybrids made up of the beginning of the future and the endings of the imperfect.

In Conversation 1, there are three examples of it:

je jouerais	I would play
(from **jouer**:	future: j**e jouer**ai imperfect: **je jou<u>ais</u>**)
je refuserais	I would refuse
(from **refuser**:	future: je **refuser**ai imperfect: **je refus<u>ais</u>**)
j'accepterais	I would accept
(from **accepter**:	future: **j'accepter**ai imperfect: **j'accept<u>ais</u>**)

Becoming an actress

Sophie

Comment envisages-tu ta carrière dans le théâtre?

Séverine

Eh bien, si je réussis un concours, je ferai d'abord la formation, et la formation dépend de l'école dans laquelle je tombe. C'est-à-dire que…chaque école a son style, que ce soit à Londres, à Paris, à Bruxelles…les écoles ont une formation différente et amènent vers un travail différent et donc des rôles aussi assez différents. Si je pouvais choisir, je jouerais des rôles pleins d'énergie, de rythme et…et de folie. J'aime beaucoup les, les femmes tourmentées et folles – folles parce qu'elles ont beaucoup souffert – donc ça c'est quand même des rôles un peu dramatiques, quand même. Ça dépendra aussi des propositions. Si on me proposait des rôles, je pense que je ne refuserais pas – j'accepterais n'importe quoi.

LISTEN FOR…	
un concours	competitive exam
la formation	training
folie	madness

VOCABULARY

la carrière	career
amener	to lead
tourmenter	to torment
folle (f. of **fou**)	mad
souffrir (past part. **souffert**)	to suffer
quand même	really, still, all the same
la proposition	offer, suggestion

si je réussis un concours, je ferai d'abord la formation if I pass a competitive examination, I shall do my training first of all. **Réussir** means 'to succeed'. **Réussir un examen** is 'to pass an exam'; **passer un examen** is 'to sit an exam'. **Concours** are the usual means of selection for professional training in France.

la formation dépend de l'école dans laquelle je tombe the training depends on the [drama] school in which I land. Notice the **de** in **dépendre de**: **Ça dépend de toi** 'That depends on you.'

C'est-à-dire que… That's to say that…

que ça soit whether that be. **Soit** is a (subjunctive) form of **être** – you don't need to use it yourself yet.

Si je pouvais choisir, je jouerais des rôles pleins d'énergie If I could choose, I would play roles full of energy. **Je pouvais**

is from the imperfect of **pouvoir**. **Je jouerais** is from the conditional tense of the verb **jouer** (future: je **jouerai** and imperfect: je **jouais**). The difference in pronunciation between **je jouerai** and **je jouerais** is very slight – so slight that some French people have trouble making the distinction between them.

Si on me proposait des rôles, je pense que je ne refuserais pas If they offered me roles, I think that I wouldn't refuse. Another example of **Si** + imperfect tense, followed by the conditional (even if **je pense que** complicates the structure). **Je refuserais** is from the conditional of **refuser** (future: je **refuserai** and imperfect: je **refusais**).

j'accepterais I'd accept. From the conditional tense of the verb **accepter** (future: j'**accepterai** and imperfect: j'**acceptais**).

n'importe quoi anything at all (literally it doesn't matter what). **N'importe qui** is 'anybody at all' and **n'importe comment** is 'any old way' (as in **Il s'habille n'importe comment** 'He dresses any old way').

(left) Séverine
(right) Sophie

PRACTICE

1

On the recording, Jean-Pierre asks Marianne
Ça va, ta carrière?   Is your career going OK?
Listen to the whole conversation a couple of times and then indicate which
of the following are true and which false:

TRUE /FALSE

a Marianne wants to join a touring company. ☐ ☐

b She has an audition with them on Monday. ☐ ☐

c She would accept any roles they offered her. ☐ ☐

d The company will tour European capitals. ☐ ☐

e They will put on innovative modern drama. ☐ ☐

f Marianne's favourite roles are comic ones. ☐ ☐

Answers p. 112

2 Write the appropriate verb from the box into each of the gaps below:

a Moi, je n'aime pas voyager, alors, si on me proposait des vacances à

Tahiti, je _____!

b Même si tu étais riche, tu ne _____

pas content!

c Si j'avais un piano, je _____

tous les soirs du Mozart!

d Je l'aime! S'il me demandait de partir en vacances avec lui, bien sûr

que j' _____!

e Si ton travail t'intéressait, tu _____

beaucoup plus!

Answers p. 112   **travaillerais   jouerais   refuserais   accepterais   serais**

3 On the recording, you are being interviewed for a job (**un poste**). You'll
need some of the verbs from Exercise 2, plus **j'aurais** 'I'd have' and the
phrase **avec plaisir** 'with pleasure'. Use **est-ce que** for your questions in the
normal way.

Philippe Monnet in the studio

What would you do if you won the lottery jackpot?

Frédéric	Que feriez-vous si vous gagniez le gros lot du Loto?
Sophie	Si je gagnais le gros lot au Loto, je m'offrirais une croisière en bateau et je ferais le tour du monde!
Pierre	Alors, si je gagnais au Loto, d'abord, je m'achèterais une voiture pour changer de ma vieille voiture, qui marche très mal, et après, je m'offrirais un très, très beau voyage.
Christine	Je crois d'abord que je mettrais l'argent à la banque, premièrement, pour me laisser le temps de réfléchir, quand même. Ensuite, je donnerais une immense fête, avec tous les gens que je connais.
Bruno	Il est difficile que je gagne au Loto, parce que je n'y joue jamais. Maintenant, si jamais cela m'arrivait, je pense que je m'achèterais peut-être un cheval…ou un avion…
Anne	Si je gagnais au Loto, j'arrêterais de travailler; comme ça, j'aurais plein de temps libre pour faire différentes activités, pour prendre le temps de vivre, pour prendre surtout le temps de ne rien faire.

> ### LISTEN FOR...
>
> | | |
> |---|---|
> | **le gros lot du/au Loto** | lottery jackpot |
> | **le tour du monde** | world tour |
> | **le temps de ne rien faire** | time to do nothing |

VOCABULARY

l'argent (m.)	money
laisser	to leave
réfléchir	to reflect, to think
la fête	(here) party (also feast, feast-day)
les gens (m.)	people
le cheval	horse
l'avion (m.)	plane

Que feriez-vous si vous gagniez le gros lot du Loto? What would you do if you won the lottery jackpot? **Vous feriez** is from the conditional of the verb **faire** (future: **vous ferez** and imperfect: **vous faisiez**). Another example of the **vous** form of the conditional: **vous habiteriez** (future: **vous habiterez** and imperfect: **vous habitiez**). **Vous gagniez** is from the imperfect of the verb **gagner**.

je m'offrirais une croisière en bateau I'd treat myself to a cruise on a ship. **Offrir** (like **donner**) means 'to give'.

je m'achèterais…, je mettrais…, je donnerais…, j'arrêterais…, j'aurais… I'd buy myself…, I'd put…, I'd give…, I'd stop…, I'd have. All conditionals, from the verbs **acheter**, **mettre**, **donner**, **arrêter** and **avoir**.

qui marche très mal which works very badly. **Marcher** is literally 'to walk', but it is also used of the functioning of a piece of equipment: **Ma montre ne marche pas** 'My watch doesn't work.'

Il est difficile que je gagne au Loto   It would be difficult for me to win the lottery. Oddly enough, Bruno doesn't use the conditional here (though he could have done): what he actually says is 'It is difficult that I win in the lottery.'

comme ça, j'aurais plein de temps libre that way, I'd have plenty of free time. **J'aurais** is from the conditional of **avoir**. **Plein de** 'plenty of/lots of' is a colloquial expression which you hear quite frequently: **plein d'amis** 'lots of friends', **plein d'argent** 'lots of money'.

pour prendre le temps de vivre   to take the time to enjoy life.

pour prendre surtout le temps de ne rien faire   above all, to take the time to do nothing. You have met sentences like **Je ne fais rien.** 'I am doing nothing.' When **ne + rien** is used with an infinitive, the infinitive comes after both of them. The same applies to **ne + pas**: **Je préfère ne pas faire le ménage.** 'I prefer not to do the housework.'

PRACTICE

4

Jacqueline and Roger also said what they'd do if they won the lottery jackpot. Listen and see if you can answer the questions.

Roger speaks of **les œuvres ou les associations**, literally 'good works or associations'; we'd use the blanket term 'charities'. You'll find the transcript with the Answers on p. 112.

a   What would Jacqueline do?

_____

b   What would the surroundings be?

_____

c   Who would come there?

_____

d   Roger says, 'It's relatively easy – one can show oneself to be generous when...'. Can you complete the sentence?

_____

e   What would he do with the money?

_____

f   What does he say the difficult question would be?

_____

g   What does he say he intends to do in order to have more chance of answering it?

Answers p. 112   _____

5 This writer would use a large windfall to help the homeless.

VOCABULARY	
bâtir	to build
le foyer	hostel
les sans-abri	the homeless (lit. those without shelter)

Si j'étais riche, si je n'avais pas besoin de gagner ma vie, je travaillerais quand même, mais ce serait un travail non payé. Je fonderais une association pour aider les sans-abri. Nous bâtirions un foyer où n'importe qui pourrait demander à être nourri et logé - ou peut-être qu'on ne le bâtirait pas, mais qu'on achèterait un ancien hôpital qu'on transformerait en foyer. Nous aurions des conseillers pour aider ces gens à trouver du travail et ensuite nous les aiderions à louer un logement permanent. Comme ça, ces personnes seraient réintégrées à la société au lieu de rester plus ou moins à la poubelle.

a See if you can identify the French terms for:

an old hospital _____

more or less in the dustbin _____

fed and housed _____

to earn my living _____

permanent accommodation _____

unpaid work _____

perhaps _____

anybody at all _____

counsellors _____

b The endings for the conditional are the same as for the imperfect: **-ais, -ais, -ait, -ions, -iez, -aient**. There are eleven examples of it in the text. See if you can underline them all and give the infinitive of each of them.

Answers p. 112

6 What about you? What would you do if you became a lottery millionaire? Daydream on paper or aloud by making up nine sentences using verbs from Conversation 2 and Exercise 4:

je m'offrirais	**je ferais**	**je m'achèterais**
je mettrais	**je donnerais**	**j'arrêterais**
j'aurais	**je pourrais**	**je serais**

7 You'll need to use some of those same verbs to tell Jean-Pierre some of the things you would like to do if you had the chance. New phrase: **écrire un roman** 'to write a novel'.

Why couldn't we send a manned flight to Mars now?

Intervieweuse

Pourquoi est-ce qu'on ne pourrait pas envoyer des hommes sur Mars maintenant?

M. Vaillant

Ben, je crois, ça serait assez difficile parce qu'on, on a plusieurs difficultés. Bon, d'une part, le voyage durerait un an, à peu près, et donc il faut quelqu'un qui ait le courage de rester un an enfermé, rester quelques jours là-bas et puis revenir encore un an, donc ça fait une mission qui serait très longue. Ensuite, il y a une deuxième raison, c'est qu'il y a beaucoup de radiations sur le chemin et, au jour d'aujourd'hui, quelqu'un qui ferait ce voyage attraperait le cancer avant d'arriver sur Mars. Donc, pour y arriver, il faudra trouver des protections pas trop lourdes permettant de se protéger des radiations. Et puis, également, avant d'envoyer des hommes, on veut envoyer des engins mécaniques pour savoir exactement ce qu'on va trouver.

VOCABULARY

assez	quite
difficile	difficult
la difficulté	difficulty
plusieurs	several
d'une part	on the one hand
à peu près	approximately
la raison	reason
sur le chemin	on the way
se protéger de	to protect oneself from

serait…, durerait…, ferait…, attraperait… would be…, would last…, would make…, would catch. All conditionals.

il faut quelqu'un qui ait le courage de rester un an enfermé you need someone who has the courage to remain shut up for a year. The subjunctive **ait** (from **avoir**) indicates that this is a hypothetical person: yet again, you don't need to use it yourself at this stage. **Enfermé** is, not surprisingly, from the verb **enfermer**.

puis revenir encore un an then to come back (which would take) another year.

au jour d'aujourd'hui at the present time. It is simpler just to say **aujourd'hui**.

avant d'arriver sur Mars…, avant d'envoyer des hommes before arriving on Mars…, before sending men. A reminder of the construction

avant de + infinitive before + ……-ing

pour y arriver in order to arrive there.

pour savoir in order to know. Note the use of **pour** meaning 'in order to'.

il faudra trouver des protections pas trop lourdes it will be necessary to find forms of protection which are not too heavy.

ce qu'on va trouver what we're going to find (literally that which one is going to find).

8

You are fast becoming an expert on Mars, so see if you can answer Marianne's questions on it with a bit of help from Philippe. Most of the language is in Conversation 3. You may like to be reminded of **l'aller** 'the outward journey', **le retour** 'the return part of the journey' and **seulement** 'only'. The conditional of **il y a** is **il y aurait** 'there would be'.

9

On the recording, a member of a trade union (**un syndicat**) tries to persuade one of its officials that the union ought to send a representative to the International Congress (**le Congrès International**).

What three reasons does the (male) official give for not sending anyone? How does his (female) colleague counter them?

His reasons   *Her counter-arguments*

a _____   _____
   _____   _____
   _____   _____

b _____   _____
   _____   _____
   _____   _____

c _____   _____
   _____   _____
   _____   _____

Answers p. 112

10 What would a better world be like? See what you make of this text – you can express your opinion by responding to the questionnaire below it.

VOCABULARY			
digne	dignified, worthy	**gagner (sa) vie**	to earn (one's) living
la parole	word	**concitoyen** (m.)	fellow citizen
l'évêque (m.)	bishop	**l'impôt** (m.)	tax
le corps social	society (literally social body)	**élevé(e)**	high, raised
prêt(e)	ready		

You can, of course, look up in the vocabulary at the back of the book any other words that you don't remember or can't guess.

Allô? Vous m'entendez?

Dans une société juste, personne n'aurait faim, personne ne serait sans abri. La vie de tous serait digne et libre. Chacun travaillerait dans la mesure de ses possibilités, et tout travail serait récompensé avec justice.

Pourquoi est-ce que ces paroles nous semblent utopiques? Pourquoi est-ce que ce ne serait qu'un rêve d'envisager un monde meilleur? Et pourquoi surtout avons-nous la réaction 'Ce n'est pas intéressant' lorsqu'on en parle? La Commission Sociale des Évêques de France a dit: 'Le silence sur un projet de société révèle une sorte de paralysie du corps social tout entier.'

– Vous et moi, sommes-nous paralysés?
– Voudrions-nous voter pour des réformes sociales?
– Serions-nous prêts à gagner un peu moins bien notre vie si cela permettait de redonner vie à bon nombre de nos concitoyens?

Et si jamais nous étions prêts, encore faudrait-il trouver un parti politique intéressé et capable de réaliser une renaissance sociale digne du nom.

Allô? Vous m'entendez?

QUESTIONNAIRE

a A votre avis, est-ce que la société actuelle est juste?

OUI / NON / JE NE SAIS PAS

b Etes-vous d'accord que 'Le silence sur un projet de société révèle une sorte de paralysie du corps social tout entier'?

OUI / NON / JE NE SAIS PAS

c Avez-vous l'impression d'être vous-même paralysé(e) vis-à-vis des inégalités sociales?

OUI / NON / JE NE SAIS PAS

d Voteriez-vous pour des réformes sociales si vous deviez payer des impôts plus élevés?

OUI / NON / JE NE SAIS PAS

e A votre avis, existe-t-il dans votre pays un parti politique capable de réaliser une vraie renaissance sociale?

OUI / NON / JE NE SAIS PAS

la carrière	career

si je réussis un concours,
   je ferai la formation
	if I pass a competitive exam,
	   I shall do the training

ça dépendra (de)	it will depend (on)

si on me proposait des rôles,
   j'accepterais
   n'importe quoi
	if they offered me roles,
	   I would accept
	   anything at all

n'importe qui	anybody at all
n'importe comment	any old how
souffrir (past part. souffert)	to suffer

que feriez-vous
   si vous gagniez
   le gros lot du Loto?
	what would you do
	   if you won
	   the Lottery jackpot?

si je gagnais,
   je ferais
   le tour du monde
	if I won,
	   I'd do
	   a world tour

quand même	really, still, all the same
la fête	party, feast, feast-day
les gens (m.)	people
le cheval	horse
l'avion (m.)	plane
je mettrais l'argent à la banque	I'd put the money in the bank
j'arrêterais de travailler	I'd stop working
le temps de ne rien faire	time to do nothing

pourquoi est-ce qu'on
   ne pourrait pas
   (+ infinitive) …?
	why
	   couldn't we …?

ça serait assez difficile	that would be rather difficult
il y aurait plusieurs difficultés	there would be several difficulties
le voyage durerait un an	the trip would last a year

on attraperait le cancer
   avant d'arriver sur Mars
	they would get (literally catch) cancer
	   before arriving on Mars

d'une part	on the one hand
à peu près	approximately
la raison	reason
sur le chemin	on the way
se protéger de	to protect oneself from

GRAMMAR AND EXERCISES

Si...

There are two basic sentence patterns with **si**/if:
- If X happen**s**, Y **will** happen.
- If X happen**ed**, Y **would** happen.

In grammatical terms, the constructions are:
- **Si** + present ▷ future
- **Si** + imperfect ▷ conditional

Si + present ▷ future

This is the most straightforward sort of 'if', describing something which is a distinct possibility:

S'il fait beau, je ferai ma lessive.
If it is fine, I shall do my washing.

Si vous écrivez au directeur, il vous répondra.
If you write to the director, he will reply to you.

Si tu viens avant huit heures, nous pourrons aller au cinéma.
If you come before eight o'clock, we shall be able to go to the cinema.

11 Choose the correct verbs from the boxes to help you translate:

a If I am ill, I shall stay in bed.

> **je suis / je serai / je serais...malade**
> **je reste / je resterai / je resterais... au lit**

b If it rains, we shall not go out.

> **il pleut / il pleuvra / il pleuvrait**
> **nous ne sortons pas / nous ne sortirons pas / nous ne sortirions pas**

c If the children go to the swimming pool, they will be happy.

> **les enfants vont / iront / iraient...à la piscine**
> **ils sont / seront / seraient...contents**

d We'll have dinner together, if you wish.

> **nous dînons / nous dînerons / nous dînerions...ensemble**
> **vous voulez / vous voudrez / vous voudriez**

e If Patrick learns English, he will go to England with the school.

> **apprend / apprendra / apprendrait...l'anglais**
> **il va / il ira / il irait...en Angleterre avec l'école**

Answers p. 112

Si + imperfect ▷ conditional

This is a more hypothetical or tentative sort of 'if':

Si j'étais Président de la République, je créerais des milliers d'emplois.
If I were President of the Republic, I would create thousands of jobs.

Si tu cessais de fumer, tu risquerais moins d'attraper le cancer.
If you stopped smoking, you would be at less risk of getting cancer.

Ton travail serait plus intéressant si tu changeais de poste.
Your work would be more interesting if you changed job.

The conditional looks like this:

j'habiterais	**nous habiterions**
tu habiterais	**vous habiteriez**
il habiterait	**ils habiteraient**
elle habiterait	**elles habiteraient**

The beginning of the word is the same as the beginning of the future form and the ending is the same as in the imperfect.

You may find it helpful to have a reminder of some of the verbs where the future – and therefore the conditional – has an irregular beginning.

Infinitive	*Conditional*	
être	**je serais**	I would be
faire	**je ferais**	I would make/do
aller	**j'irais**	I would go
avoir	**j'aurais**	I would have
savoir	**je saurais**	I would know
vouloir	**je voudrais**	I would like
devoir	**je devrais**	I ought to
pouvoir	**je pourrais**	I could
voir	**je verrais**	I would see
envoyer	**j'enverrais**	I would send
tenir (and compounds)	**je tiendrais**	I would hold
venir (and compounds)	**je viendrais**	I would come
falloir (il faut)	**il faudrait**	it would be necessary
pleuvoir (il pleut)	**il pleuvrait**	it would rain

12 The **nous** and **vous** forms of the conditional are some of the most difficult tongue-twisters in the whole of the French language. First, write out the forms which correspond to these infinitives and then turn to the recording for help with the pronunciation.

prendre: nous _____ vous _____

habiter: nous _____ vous _____

finir: nous _____ vous _____

travailler: nous _____ vous _____

écrire: nous _____ vous _____

Answers p. 112

13 All the sentences below follow the pattern of **si** + imperfect ▷ conditional. Three options are given by each of the gaps: see if you can choose and write in the correct one.

a Si tu m' _____ vraiment, tu me _____ libre.
   aimeras / aimais / aimerais   *laisseras / laissais / laisserais*

b Si vous _____ à l'école, vous _____ parler au professeur.
   irez / alliez / iriez   *pourrez / pouviez / pourriez*

c Si nous _____ mieux le français, nous _____ au théâtre.
   comprendrons / comprenions / comprendrions   *irons / allions / irions*

d Si tous nos petits-enfants _____ à la maison en même temps, nous
                  _____ pas assez de place.
   viendront / venaient / viendraient   *aurons / avions / aurions*

e Si on _____ Georges, il _____ content.
   invitera / invitait / inviterait   *sera / était /serait*

f Si tu _____ gentil, tu _____ la vaisselle de temps en temps.
   seras / étais / serais   *feras / faisais / ferais*

Answers p. 112

14 Below is part of a letter sent to a girl who had applied for a job as an au pair. See if you can fill in the gaps with the conditional corresponding to each of the infinitives.

Mademoiselle,

Je vous remercie de votre lettre. Je [vouloir] _____ vous donner quelques renseignements supplémentaires sur les conditions d'emploi et ce que nous attendons d'une jeune fille au pair. Si vous veniez chez nous...

■ vous [avoir] _____ une chambre individuelle.

■ vous [devoir] _____ vous occuper de Carine (7 ans): vous l'[accompagner]

   _____ à l'école le matin et vous [aller] _____ la chercher

   l'après-midi. Vous [être] _____ donc libre de 9h jusqu'à 16h 30 tous les jours

   et vous [pouvoir] _____ suivre des cours de français en ville.

■ vous [venir] _____ passer les week-ends avec nous dans notre résidence

   secondaire en montagne: là, vous [faire] _____ le ménage. (En ville, c'est la

   femme de ménage qui s'en occupe.)

■ vous [avoir] _____ une journée de liberté par semaine, mais il [falloir]

   _____ être prête à varier le jour, en fonction de mon travail. Je ne [savoir]

   _____ mon emploi du temps qu'une semaine à l'avance.

Answers p. 112

AND FINALLY...

15 A game that is a cross between Consequences and fortune cookies! It is best played with a partner, but you can do both halves yourself if you are following the course on your own.

On separate slips of paper, Partner A writes a series of conditions like

- **Si vous travaillez bien**
- **Si vous apprenez le français**
- **Si vous buvez trop**

(all in the present tense).

Again on separate slips of paper, Partner B writes a series of fortune-telling predictions like

- **Vous serez riche**
- **Vous aurez dix enfants**
- **Vous ferez le tour du monde**

(all in the future tense).

Each pile of slips of paper is then shuffled and one condition and one prediction drawn at random. They are read out in sequence
(e.g. **Si vous buvez trop, vous aurez dix enfants!**).

Stage 2 of the game uses the same set of conditions and predictions, newly shuffled. This time when you draw them, the task is to convert them into a hypothetical If + imperfect ▷ conditional.
(e.g. If you draw **Si vous buvez trop** + **vous aurez dix enfants**, what you say is: **Si vous buviez trop, vous auriez dix enfants**).

The recording gives some samples of how the two parts of this exercise might work out.

EXERCISE 1

(a) True **(b)** False **(c)** True **(d)** True **(e)** False
(f) False

EXERCISE 2

refuserais / serais / jouerais / accepterais /
travaillerais

EXERCISE 4

(a) Have a big house built **(b)** Countryside, fields, a
forest near by **(c)** The children, the grandchildren
and lots of friends **(d)** one has not really won
(e) Give it away **(f)** Would he be able to choose
wisely the people and particularly the charities he
gave it to? **(g)** Play the lottery regularly!

Transcript
Jacqueline

Si je gagnais le gros lot du Loto, je pense que je
ferais construire une très grande maison, une
belle maison au milieu de la campagne, au milieu
des champs, près d'une forêt, où je pourrais
recevoir nos enfants, nos petits-enfants et
beaucoup d'amis.

Roger

Bon, c'est, c'est relativement facile – on peut se
montrer généreux quand on ne l'a pas gagné
réellement. Je, je crois que je m'en servirais pour
le distribuer, le donner…et la question profonde
serait 'Est-ce que je serais capable de bien choisir
les personnes et surtout les œuvres ou les
associations auxquelles je le donnerais?' Je ne
sais pas; c'est une, c'est une question difficile.
C'est une question difficile, mais pour avoir plus
de chances de vous répondre, je vais commencer
à, à jouer régulièrement au Loto!

EXERCISE 5

(a) un ancien hôpital / plus ou moins à la poubelle /
nourri et logé / gagner ma vie / un logement
permanent / un travail non payé / peut-être /
n'importe qui / des conseillers **(b)** travaillerais
(travailler) / serait (être) / fonderais (fonder)/ bâtirions
(bâtir) / pourrais (pouvoir) / bâtirait (bâtir) / achèterait
(acheter) / transformerait (transformer) / aurions
(avoir) / aiderions (aider) / seraient (être)

EXERCISE 9

(a) It would be very expensive. / The union would
pay. **(b)** One would need to get a visa –
complicated! / Not that complicated! **(c)** They will
be speaking English at the Congress. / The fact that
the official does not speak English himself is not a
reason for not sending anyone.

EXERCISE 11

(a) je suis / je resterai **(b)** il pleut / nous ne
sortirons pas **(c)** vont / seront **(d)** nous dînerons
/ vous voulez **(e)** apprend / il ira

EXERCISE 12

nous prendrions, vous prendriez / nous habiterions,
vous habiteriez / nous finirions, vous finiriez / nous
travaillerions, vous travailleriez / nous écririons, vous
écririez

EXERCISE 13

(a) aimais / laisserais **(b)** alliez / pourriez
(c) comprenions / irions **(e)** venaient / aurions
(e) invitait / serait **(f)** étais / ferais

EXERCISE 14

voudrais / auriez / devriez / accompagneriez / iriez /
seriez / pourriez / viendriez / feriez / auriez / faudrait /
saurais

8

MAKING PROPOSALS

WHAT YOU WILL LEARN

▶ suggesting social activities
▶ responding to others' suggestions
▶ telephone language
▶ making a business appointment

POINTS TO REMEMBER

You have already met much of the language you need for making proposals and saying what you think ought to happen:

On peut + infinitive:

On peut venir	We can come

On pourrait + infinitive:

On pourrait partir	We could leave

On doit + infinitive:

On doit parler	We must speak

On devrait + infinitive:

On devrait attendre	We ought to wait

Il faut + infinitive:

Il faut y aller	We must go there

Il faudrait + infinitive:

Il faudrait rester	We ought to stay
Ça te dit? / Ça vous dit?	Do you fancy that?
Ça te dirait? / Ça vous dirait?	Would you fancy that?

BEFORE YOU BEGIN

When you start a foreign language, progress can be exhilarating: you go from 0 to 60 words in next to no time, and 60 words are infinitely more than you knew before you began, so you feel you are soaring up a steep learning curve. It is ironic that, as you get better at the language, you often have the impression of sliding backwards down the curve. One of the reasons for this is that, when you have met thousands of words – and they combine in all sorts of unpredictable ways – you are bound to forget very basic things from time to time. The only sensible advice is to be patient with yourself and keep working at the language because you are almost certainly making more progress than you realise.

CONVERSATION 1

Discussing how to spend Sunday afternoon

Pierre	Anne, as-tu prévu quelque chose pour dimanche après-midi?
Anne	Non, non, j'ai pas de projets particuliers – je pensais rester chez moi.
Pierre	Nous pourrions peut-être aller faire un tennis ensemble?
Anne	Oh, là, là! Tu sais que je joue très, très mal au tennis!
Pierre	Ah, oui! J'avais oublié.
Anne	Moi, j'aimerais mieux aller me promener au bord du canal – ça te dit?
Pierre	Oui, pourquoi pas? Moi, je préférerais, à ce moment-là, aller faire un tour à la foire artisanale à côté de chez moi.
Anne	Ah, oui! Oui, oui, oui.
Pierre	C'est très intéressant; en plus, il y a une exposition de peintures en même temps.
Anne	D'accord, oui, oui, ça me va.
Pierre	Oui?
Anne	Très bien.
Pierre	OK.

LISTEN FOR...

au bord du canal	on the bank of the canal
la foire artisanale	craft fair
une exposition de peintures	exhibition of paintings

VOCABULARY

le tennis	tennis, game of tennis, tennis court
ensemble	together
se promener	to go for a walk
pourquoi pas?	why not?
ça me va	that suits me

as-tu prévu quelque chose...? have you planned anything...? **Prévoir**, literally 'to foresee', is used in this sense of having something in mind.

j'ai pas de projets particuliers I have no special plans.

je pensais rester chez moi I was thinking (imperfect tense) of staying at home. The French construction does not have an equivalent of the English 'of' and uses an infinitive where English has a form in -ing. There will be more about this in the Grammar section.

Nous pourrions peut-être aller faire un tennis ensemble? Perhaps we could (conditional tense) go and have a game of tennis together? Keep an eye out for **aller +** infinitive in this unit: it corresponds to the English 'to go and (do something)'.

je joue très, très mal au tennis! I play tennis very, very badly! A reminder that it is **jouer à +** a game and **jouer de +** a musical instrument: **jouer au tennis** but **jouer du piano**.

J'avais oublié I had forgotten. **J'ai oublié** means 'I have forgotten'. **J'avais oublié** puts it further in the past (**j'avais** = I had).

j'aimerais mieux I'd prefer (literally I'd like better). This is exactly the same as **je préférerais**. Both are conditionals.

à ce moment-là in that case (i.e. if you don't want to play tennis).

aller faire un tour à la foire artisanale à côté de chez moi to go round the craft fair by my place. **Un artisan** is 'a craftsperson' and **l'artisanat** is 'handicrafts'. The adjective **artisanal** implies traditional, old-fashioned skill; it is often applied to hand-made bread: **le pain artisanale**.

PRACTICE

1 See if you can find in Conversation 1 different phrases which mean roughly the same as:

a près de ma maison _____

b j'avais l'intention de rester à la maison _____

_____

c OK _____

d as-tu des projets? _____

e je préférerais _____

Answers p. 128   f ça te va? _____

2 On the recording, Marianne and Jean-Pierre arrange to spend an afternoon together.

a On which day are they planning to go out?

_____

b Where does Marianne suggest they go?

_____

c Why is Jean-Pierre not keen?

_____

d Where does Jean-Pierre first suggest they go?

_____

e Why is Marianne not keen? (2 reasons)

_____

f What do they finally agree on?

Answers p. 128

_____

3 Try to arrange an outing with Marianne for this Sunday. Your lines are in the speech balloons – select the right one to match each of Philippe's prompts.

> *Au bord du canal, peut-être?*

> *Il y a une exposition des peintures de Picasso.*

> *As-tu prévu quelque chose pour dimanche après-midi?*

> *Nous pourrions aller nous promener...*

> *Alors, nous pourrions aller voir l'exposition de peintures.*

When you have done the exercise, you could try it again without looking at the speech balloons.

CONSERVATION 2

Arranging to go to the cinema

Sandrine	Sophie, qu'est-ce que tu fais ce soir? Tu n'as pas envie de sortir?
Sophie	Ça dépend – pour quoi faire?
Sandrine	Je sais pas – on peut aller au cinéma?
Sophie	Oui – mais à quelle heure?
Sandrine	Je sais pas – la séance de huit heures?
Sophie	Huit heures...d'accord. Et puis on irait voir quoi?
Sandrine	Voilà, c'est la question: t'as envie de voir quoi?
Sophie	Je sais pas. Actuellement, il y a *Phénomène*.
Sandrine	*Phénomène?*
Sophie	Oui, tu sais, avec John Travolta...
Sandrine	Ah, moi j'ai entendu parler de...*Independence Day*...
Sophie	Bof...Quoique...Pourquoi pas?
Sandrine	On va voir ça?
Sophie	D'accord. Alors, on se donne rendez-vous où?
Sandrine	Je sais pas – au petit café qui est à côté du cinéma?
Sophie	Mm, oui. Heu, on se donne rendez-vous là-bas ou alors je passe chez toi?
Sandrine	T'as qu'à passer chez moi.
Sophie	D'accord. Alors, je passe chez toi à sept heures et demie et on ira boire un petit café avant d'aller au cinéma à la séance de huit heures.
Sandrine	D'accord – on fait comme ça.
Sophie	OK!
Sandrine	A tout à l'heure!
Sophie	Ciao!

LISTEN FOR...

tu n'as pas envie de sortir?	don't you fancy going out?
pour quoi faire?	in order to do what?
la séance	showing, sitting

Sophie

VOCABULARY

actuellement	at the moment
à tout à l'heure!	see you later!

pour quoi faire? in order to do what? Notice the difference between this and **pourquoi** (all one word, meaning 'why').

Quoi? 'What?' can be used on its own, though it is very informal. **Comment?** is a more polite way of saying 'What?' You are generally safer saying **Pardon?** 'Sorry?', 'Pardon?'

on irait voir quoi? what would we go and see? (literally one would go to see what?).

j'ai entendu parler de... I've heard people talking about... (literally I have heard [to] tell of...). Note the infinitive (**parler**) where English has a form in -ing. Further example:

Je l'ai vu travailler I have seen him working

Bof...Quoique... **Bof** is a dismissive noise and **quoique** 'although' is the beginning of a sentence that Sophie does not continue.

on se donne rendez-vous où? where shall we arrange to meet?

T'as qu'à passer chez moi Just come via my place. This is a colloquial reduction of **Tu n'as qu'à...** (literally You have only to...). Further examples of **ne...que**: **Je n'ai qu'une semaine** 'I only have a week'; **Vous n'avez qu'à demander** 'You have only to ask.'

4 You will need to reuse the language from Conversation 2 as you arrange to go out to the cinema with Marianne.

5 Or maybe you prefer to stay home and watch a video? See what you make of this one! **Un petit ami** is a boyfriend and **la chasse** is the hunt.

VIDÉO

Où sont les hommes?

Whitney Houston   Angela Bassett

Où~ Sont les Hommes?

Après Bodyguard, Whitney Houston dans une comédie tendrement drôle.

Changement de décor. Après avoir réalisé *Good Morning Vietnam*, Forest Whitaker vous entraîne dans la vie amoureuse de quatre femmes. Bernadine (Angela Bassett) est en plein divorce. Gloria n'a qu'une seule compagnie: son fils de dix-sept ans. Robin, elle, a le don de tomber sur des cas très spéciaux. Quant à Savannah (Whitney Houston), elle retombe sur son ex-petit ami, malheureusement marié. Rien de très positif, mais nos quatre copines sont convaincues que l'homme parfait existe...La chasse est ouverte!

a Who directed this film?

_____

b Who meets up with an old boyfriend?

_____

c What's the problem with him?

_____

d Who has the gift of landing weirdos?

_____

e Who lives with Gloria?

_____

f The hunt is on...but what is the quarry?

_____

`Answers p. 128`

6 All the answers to the crossword have already occurred in this unit, though, in the case of verbs, it may sometimes be as a different form of the same verb. You can ignore accents for crossword purposes.

Across

4. Desire (5)
7. I'd like better (1, 8, 5)
11. Not (2)
13. Then (4)
15. Something (7, 5)
18. This (2)
19. Had (2)
20. There is (2, 1, 1)
23. Badly (3)
24. We, they, one (2)
26. You, to you (2)
28. Why (8)
30. Is it **le** or **la cinéma**? (2)
31. At the house of (4)
33. Bank (4)
34. Nothing (4)
36. Same (4)
37. Makes (4)
39. Sunday (8)
40. Craft (adj.) (9)
42. See you later! (1, 4, 1, 1, 5)

Down

1. Is it **le** or **la café**? (2)
2. To do (5)
3. To stay (6)
4. Exhibition (10)
5. To see (4)
6. In (2)
8. At the present time (12)
9. To me (2)
10. To each other (2)
12. To be (4)
14. To play (5)
16. Is it **le** or **la tennis**? (2)
17. What (4)
21. Is it **le** or **la canal**? (2)
22. Have (you) (2)
25. Fair (5)
27. Painting (8)
29. Prefers (7)
31. That (2)
32. Thinks (5)
33. Well (4)
35. Would go (5)
38. Goes, suits (2)
41. Is it **le** or **la séance**? (2)

CONVERSATION 3

Telephoning to arrange a business meeting

Standardiste	Entreprise GVS – bonjour!
Jacqueline	Bonjour, Madame.
Standardiste	Bonjour, Madame.
Jacqueline	Pourrais-je parler à Monsieur Frédéric Dupont, s'il vous plaît?
Standardiste	Oui – c'est de la part de qui, s'il vous plaît?
Jacqueline	De la part de Madame Ravignac.
Standardiste	Un instant – je vais voir s'il est disponible... Je vous le passe!
Jacqueline	Merci.
Frédéric	Bonjour, Jacqueline!
Jacqueline	Bonjour, Frédéric! Comment vas-tu?
Frédéric	Très bien – et toi-même?
Jacqueline	Très bien, merci.
Frédéric	Quel bon vent t'amène?
Jacqueline	Eh bien, je t'appelais au sujet du dossier Alpha.
Frédéric	Oh! c'est vrai – il faut qu'on en parle. Quel jour te convient?
Jacqueline	Mercredi, si tu veux?
Frédéric	Mercredi, oui...à 15h 30?
Jacqueline	15h 30, c'est bon.
Frédéric	Très bien.

LISTEN FOR...

c'est de la part de qui?	who is speaking?
je vous le passe!	I'll put you through to him
au sujet du dossier Alpha	regarding the Alpha project (literally file, dossier)

Telephone language:

Pourrais-je parler à... Could I speak to...

c'est de la part de qui? who is calling? (literally it is on behalf of whom?) – to which the answer is:

De la part de... It's...

Je vous le passe! I'll put you through (literally I am passing him to you).

Quel bon vent t'amène? To what do I owe the pleasure? (literally What good wind brings you?).

il faut qu'on en parle we need to talk about it (literally it is necessary that one of it talks). 'To talk <u>about</u> something' is **parler <u>de</u> quelque chose**.

VOCABULARY

le/la standardiste	switchboard operator
l'entreprise (f.)	firm
toi-même	yourself

Quel jour te convient? Which day suits you? From the verb **convenir**: **Est-ce que cela vous convient?** 'Does that suit you?'

Ça me convient parfaitement 'That suits me perfectly.'

Jacqueline

7 You need to make a business call to Madame Lenoir.
- First, negotiate your way past the switchboard!
- Then arrange a meeting with Madame Lenoir to discuss a project by the name of Cool (**le dossier Cool**).

8 The telephone call in Conversation 3 continues in the recording for this exercise. In this part of the call, they decide which of them will take responsibility for preparing each of the different aspects of the project between now and their meeting (**d'ici là** 'from now till then'). You won't understand every word, but see if you can catch the following:

a Which of them will be working on

    i. quality control? _____

    ii. contact with firms? _____

    iii. the budget? _____

    iv. planning? _____

b Do they expect to get it into final form in the course of the afternoon?

c How soon is the deadline for submitting a project (**pour remettre un dossier**)?

_____

Answers p. 128

_____

Unit 8   Making proposals

9 Here is the transcript of the recording in the last exercise. Listen again and see if you can fill in the gaps.

Frédéric	D'ici là, il nous _____ travailler dessus. _____ t'occuper de l'aspect budget?
Jacqueline	Oui.
Frédéric	Du contact avec les entreprises?
Jacqueline	_____, oui.
Frédéric	De mon côté, je, j'étudierai donc la partie planning, de même que le contrôle de qualité.
Jacqueline	_____
Frédéric	Cela nous _____ donc de finaliser ce dossier dans le courant de l'après-midi. Quelle est la date à laquelle on _____ le remettre?
Jacqueline	Oh, dans trois _____, environ.
Frédéric	Trois semaines. Oui, cela nous laisse le _____ suffisant...
Jacqueline	Oui.
Frédéric	... pour remettre un dossier dans une forme valable. Donc, à _____ prochain!
Jacqueline	A mercredi, Frédéric!
Frédéric	Je te remercie de ton appel. A _____! Au revoir!
Jacqueline	Au revoir!

When you have filled in the gaps, see if you can find in the transcript the phrases for:

a in the course of the afternoon

_____

b can you take care of...?

_____

c thank you for your call

_____

d that leaves us enough time

_____

e I shall study

Answers p. 128

_____

KEY WORDS
AND PHRASES

as-tu/avez-vous prévu quelque chose?	have you planned anything?
je n'ai pas de projets particuliers	I have no special plans
je pensais rester chez moi	I was thinking of staying at home
nous pourrions peut-être aller faire un tennis ensemble?	perhaps we could go and play a game of tennis together?
moi, je préférerais	I'd prefer
moi, j'aimerais mieux aller me promener au bord du canal	I'd prefer to go for a walk on the bank of the canal
ça te/vous dit?	do you fancy that?
oui, pourquoi pas?	yes, why not?
ça me va	that suits me
c'est très intéressant	it is very interesting
qu'est-ce que tu fais/vous faites ce soir?	what are you doing tonight?
tu n'as pas/vous n'avez pas envie de sortir?	don't you fancy going out?
ça dépend – pour quoi faire?	that depends – to do what?
la séance de huit heures	the 8 o'clock showing
on irait voir quoi?	what would we go and see?
tu as/vous avez envie de voir quoi?	what do you fancy seeing?
j'ai entendu parler de…	I've heard people talking about…
on va voir ça?	shall we go and see that?
on se donne rendez-vous où?	where shall we meet?
je passe chez toi/vous?	shall I come via your place?
tu n'as qu'à passer chez moi	just come via my place
on ira boire un petit café	we'll go and have a quick coffee
on fait comme ça	that's what we'll do
à tout à l'heure!	see you later!
une entreprise	a firm
pourrais-je parler à…	could I speak to…?
c'est de la part de qui?	who is speaking?
de la part de…	it's…
un instant	one moment
je vais voir s'il est disponible	I'll see if he is free
je vous le passe	I'll put you through
comment vas-tu/allez-vous?	how are you?
quel bon vent t'/vous amène?	to what do I owe the pleasure?
je t'/vous appelais au sujet du dossier Alpha	I was calling you regarding the Alpha project
c'est vrai	it's true
quel jour te/vous convient?	which day suits you?

More about the infinitive

The infinitive is the part of the verb which ends in **-er**, **-re** or **-ir**. In English, the infinitive is the form of the verb beginning with 'to' (to hear, to walk, to be, etc.).

10   Have another look at these phrases and sentences from the recordings in this unit and see if you can underline all the infinitives – some sentences have more than one!

a   Je pensais rester chez moi.
b   Nous pourrions peut-être aller faire un tennis ensemble?
c   Moi, j'aimerais mieux aller me promener.
d   Moi, je préférerais aller faire un tour.
e   On peut aller au cinéma?
f   Et puis on irait voir quoi?
g   On va voir ça?
h   On ira boire un petit café avant d'aller au cinéma.
i   Pourrais-je parler à Monsieur Frédéric Dupont?
j   D'ici là, il nous faut travailler dessus.
k   Peux-tu t'occuper de l'aspect budget?
l   Quelle est la date à laquelle on doit le remettre?

| Answers p. 128 |

That exercise points to one of the most useful rules in French grammar:

When there are two verbs together, the second one is always an infinitive.

The only exception is when the first of the verbs is a part of **avoir** or **être** (e.g. j'**ai fait**, il **est allé**).

11   See if you can fill in the missing word to make each of the French sentences a translation of the English:

a   Je pensais _____ au cinéma.
     I was thinking of going to the cinema.

b   Moi, j'aimerais mieux _____ chez moi.
     I'd prefer to stay at home.

c   Nous pourrions peut-être _____ _____ ça?
     Perhaps we could go and see that?

d   On doit _____ dessus.
     We ought to work on it.

e   On ira _____ au directeur.
     We shall go and speak to the director.

f   Il faut _____ le dossier dans trois semaines.
     We have to submit the project in three weeks.

| Answers p. 128 |

The verbs which are most often followed by another in this way include **pouvoir**, **vouloir**, **savoir**, **devoir** and **falloir** (**il faut**):

Pourriez-vous nous aider, s'il vous plaît?
Could you help us, please?

Qu'est-ce que vous voulez faire?
What do you want to do?

Savez-vous nager?
Can you swim? (**Savoir** is used rather than **pouvoir** when talking about skills like swimming or reading.)

Vous devez remettre le dossier avant le 6 mai.
You should submit the project before 6 May.

Vous avez dû laisser votre portefeuille dans la voiture.
You must have left your wallet in the car.

Il faut en parler avec vos collègues.
You should talk about it with your colleagues.

As **pouvoir**, **vouloir**, **savoir**, **devoir** and **falloir** are irregular verbs, it would be helpful at this point if you had a look at the different forms of them set out on p. 197.

12 This time using **tu** for 'you', see if you can translate the following sentences:

a Can you read?

---

b What do you want to see?

---

c You should talk about it with your parents. (Use **il faut**.)

---

d You should submit the project before 6 June. (Use **devoir**.)

---

e Could you help me, please?

---

f You must have left your book in your bedroom.

Answers p. 128

AND FINALLY...

13 If you look back to the transcript of Conversation 3, you will find that the language in it is particularly useful. The recording for this exercise consists of a reconstruction of Conversation 3 without Jacqueline's lines. The idea is that you should go through it several times, at first reading Jacqueline's part aloud in the pauses and, by the time you finish, saying her part from memory. If you are working with a partner, you can roleplay the conversation and then improvise a similar one with variations of your own.

14 You have a French guest spending a day with you. You want to take him out to somewhere that he will enjoy, so work out how to propose some of the possibilities in your area. On the recording, you can hear Marianne discussing with her guest how he would like to spend the day – their conversation might give you some ideas. If you are working with a partner, you can act out a similar conversation yourselves, taking it in turn to play the French visitor.

EXERCISE 1

(a) à côté de chez moi **(b)** je pensais rester chez moi **(c)** d'accord **(d)** as-tu prévu quelque chose? **(e)** j'aimerais mieux **(f)** ça te dit?

EXERCISE 2

(a) Saturday **(b)** The swimming pool
(c) There are too many people on Saturdays
(d) The new exhibition of paintings at the town hall
(e) She has already seen it – and it was not very interesting anyway **(f)** Going for a walk in the castle park

EXERCISE 5

(a) Forest Whitaker **(b)** Savannah **(c)** He is married **(d)** Robin **(e)** Her seventeen-year-old son **(f)** The perfect man!

EXERCISE 6

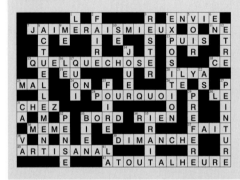

EXERCISE 8

(a) i. Frédéric ii. Jacqueline iii. Jacqueline iv. Frédéric **(b)** Yes **(c)** About three weeks

EXERCISE 9

faut / Peux-tu / Également / D'accord / permettra / doit / semaines / temps / mercredi / bientôt
(a) dans le courant de l'après-midi **(b)** peux-tu t'occuper de…? **(c)** je te remercie de ton appel
(d) cela nous laisse le temps suffisant
(e) j'étudierai

EXERCISE 10

(a) rester **(b)** aller / faire **(c)** aller / (me) promener **(d)** aller / faire **(e)** aller **(f)** voir
(g) voir **(h)** boire / aller **(i)** parler
(j) travailler **(k)** (t')occuper **(l)** remettre

EXERCISE 11

(a) aller **(b)** rester **(c)** aller voir **(d)** travailler **(e)** parler **(f)** remettre

EXERCISE 12

(a) Sais-tu lire? **(b)** Qu'est-ce que tu veux voir? **(c)** Il faut en parler avec tes parents. **(d)** Tu dois remettre le dossier avant le 6 juin. **(e)** Pourrais-tu m'aider, s'il te plaît? **(f)** Tu as dû laisser ton livre dans ta chambre.

9 | NO PROBLEM!

WHAT YOU WILL LEARN
- ▶ asking for help
- ▶ explaining problems with machines and equipment
- ▶ discussing what to do when your car won't start
- ▶ reporting lost property

POINTS TO REMEMBER

Many different forms of verbs occur in this unit – none of them new. If you want to remind yourself of how they go, you can look back to

- ■ Unit 1 for forms like **j'ai fait** (the perfect)
- ■ Unit 5 for forms like **faites!** (the imperative)
- ■ Unit 6 for forms like **je ferai** (the future)
- ■ Unit 8 for the use of **devoir** (**je dois**) + infinitive

BEFORE YOU BEGIN

You are bound to have difficulties of one kind or another when you travel, but people are usually happy to help if you know how to ask:

- ■ **Pourriez-vous m'aider, s'il vous plaît?**

and how to explain what the problem is:

■ **X ne marche pas**	X doesn't work
■ **Y ne démarre pas**	Y won't start
■ **Z est en panne**	Z has broken down

or

■ **j'ai perdu...**	I have lost...
■ **j'ai oublié...**	I have forgotten...
■ **j'ai laissé...**	I have left...
■ **on m'a volé...**	someone has stolen my...

SORTIE de SECOURS

A foreign credit card at an automatic petrol station

Anglaise	Pardon, Monsieur, pourriez-vous m'aider, s'il vous plaît?
Français	Oui? Qu'est-ce-qui vous arrive?
Anglaise	La machine n'accepte pas ma carte...
Français	Ben, attendez – on va voir ce qui se passe...
Anglaise	Merci beaucoup, hein... C'est peut-être parce que les cartes britanniques n'ont pas de puce...
Français	Ah, oui, puisqu'on doit mettre un code.
Anglaise	Ah! Mais il y a pas d'autres stations-service ouvertes aujourd'hui?
Français	Ah, je crois qu'elles sont toutes fermées aujourd'hui – c'est fête...
Anglaise	Bon...écoutez, Monsieur, j'ai de l'argent en espèces...est-ce-que je pourrais vous donner vingt euros? Est-ce que vous voudriez bien mettre votre carte à vous? Je, je, je vous donnerai les, l'argent en liquide.
Français	Ah oui, on peut faire comme ça, si vous voulez...
Anglaise	Oh, c'est très gentil.
Français	Qu'est-ce que, qu'est ce que vous voulez comme carburant?
Anglaise	Pour vingt euros?
Français	Pour vingt euros – mais de quoi? D'essence? De super? De gasoil?
Anglaise	De super, s'il vous plaît.
Français	Alors, attendez...je prends ma carte...
Anglaise	Merci beaucoup, Monsieur – c'est vraiment très aimable.

> **LISTEN FOR...**
>
> | | |
> |---|---|
> | **pourriez-vous m'aider?** | could you help me? |
> | **les cartes britanniques** | British cards |
> | **n'ont pas de puce** | have no micro-chip |

VOCABULARY

ouvert(e)(s) (from **ouvrir**)	open
aujourd'hui	today
le carburant	fuel
l'essence (f.)	(ordinary) petrol
le gasoil	diesel
aimable	kind

pourriez-vous m'aider? could you help me? If you need to shout for help, the phrase to use is **Au secours!**

Qu'est-ce qui vous arrive? What's the problem? (literally What is happening to you?)

La machine n'accepte pas ma carte The machine doesn't accept my card. In country areas, inserting a credit card into the machine by a petrol pump is often the only way of buying petrol on a Sunday or bank holiday.

on va voir ce qui se passe we'll see what's happening. The verbs **arriver** (used above) and **se passer** both mean 'to happen'.

C'est peut-être parce que les cartes britanniques n'ont pas de puce Perhaps it is because British cards don't have a micro-chip. This is indeed the problem! **Une puce** is 'a flea' – the word has been adopted to mean a micro-chip because it is tiny. **Un marché aux puces** is a 'flea-market' and **ma puce** is used as a term of endearment to a child.

puisqu'on doit mettre un code   since you have to tap in a PIN-number. In French hotels and restaurants too, clients are often asked to tap the PIN-numbers of their cards into a hand-held credit card machine as a guarantee against fraud. This does not work unless the card has a micro-chip; so far, establishments are still willing to accept our more primitive foreign cards anyway – though having your passport to hand as an alternative guarantee would be a sensible precaution.

c'est fête   it's a (bank) holiday.

écoutez, Monsieur, j'ai de l'argent en espèces   listen, Monsieur, I have money in cash. **Écoute/écoutez** are used in this way much more often than 'listen' in

English, where we should be more likely to say 'look'. **En espèces** means the same as **en liquide** (below).

Est-ce que vous voudriez bien mettre votre carte à vous?   Would you be willing to put in *your* card? In English, we can stress words by saying them with emphasis: 'Would you try *your* card?' You can't do that in French: the stress has to be indicated by adding other words, e.g.

Votre carte à vous *Your* card
  Ma carte à moi *My* card
Vous, vous avez plusieurs cartes *You* have several cards
Moi, je n'ai pas de carte *I* don't have a card

PRACTICE

1   Listen to Jean-Pierre using a credit card to pay the bill (**l'addition**) in a restaurant.

		Yes	No
a	Does the waitress ask Jean-Pierre to tap in his PIN-number?	☐	☐
b	Does she want to see his passport?	☐	☐
c	Does she ask for his signature?	☐	☐
d	Is Jean-Pierre's card a Mastercard?	☐	☐
e	Is it French?	☐	☐
f	Does the bill include service?	☐	☐

Answers p. 144

2   In case you are ever caught in the same position as the English tourist in the Conversation, the recording gives you an opportunity to practise what you would have to say.

3 Below is advice on money given in a guide to the French island of Reunion in the Indian Ocean. **La métropole** means 'metropolitan France' (i.e. mainland European France as opposed to its Overseas Departments and Territories).

ARGENT

La **monnaie locale** est l'euro, divisé cents en euros.

Les **cartes bancaires** (surtout la VISA) sont acceptées pratiquemment partout (sauf dans les chambres et tables d'hôtes) et on peut tirer du liquide dans les mêmes conditions que dans la métropole. Les chèques de la métropole ne sont pas toujours acceptés, notamment dans les chambres d'hôtes (certains ont abusé des chèques en bois en se disant qu'avec une telle distance...). Les chèques de voyage (même en) ne sont pas non plus très bien vus. Alors n'oubliez pas votre carte de crédit!

Les **chèques de voyage (traveller's chèques)** sont acceptés, mais il est difficile de les changer dans les petites et moyennes banques. Alors prévoir d'en changer une grande quantité dans les banques les plus importantes de l'île. Présenter la carte d'identité ou le passeport.

See if you can find in the text the French equivalents of:

a small and medium-sized banks

_____

b don't forget

_____

c practically everywhere

_____

d such a distance

_____

e rooms and meals in private houses

_____

f it is difficult to change them

_____

g you can take out cash

_____

h rubber cheques (not a literal translation)

Answers p. 144

_____

Anne's car won't start

Anne	Pierre, j'ai absolument besoin d'aide.
Pierre	Que se passe-t-il?
Anne	Ma voiture ne démarre pas!
Pierre	Encore!
Anne	Et oui! Encore!
Pierre	Bon! Est-ce qu'au moins tu as pensé à faire le plein d'essence?
Anne	Bien sûr! C'est la première chose à laquelle j'ai pensé.
Pierre	Tu es sûre?
Anne	Oui!
Pierre	Bon, ben alors…il n'y a qu'une solution: ça doit être la batterie.
Anne	Tu crois?
Pierre	Ah, je ne vois que ça…Bon, heureusement, j'ai des câbles de démarrage dans ma voiture, alors, ce que je peux te proposer, c'est…je vais chercher ma voiture…
Anne	Oui…
Pierre	On essaie de relancer la, la batterie…
Anne	D'accord…
Pierre	Et après, la seule solution, c'est…il faut que tu roules, que tu roules pour essayer de recharger la batterie, et…je te conseille d'aller directement chez un garagiste.
Anne	D'accord.

LISTEN FOR…

faire le plein d'essence	to fill it up with petrol
des câbles de démarrage	jump-leads
recharger la batterie	to recharge the battery

VOCABULARY

l'aide (f.)	help
au moins	at least

Que se passe-t-il? What's the matter? (literally What is happening?)

Ma voiture ne démarre pas! My car won't start! Another useful phrase is **Ma voiture est en panne** 'My car has broken down.' **Etre en panne d'essence** is 'to have run out of petrol'.

Encore! Again! **Encore** can also mean 'still' or 'yet'.

C'est la première chose à laquelle j'ai pensé It's the first thing I thought of (literally It is the first thing to which I thought). To think <u>of</u> (someone/ something) is **penser <u>à</u>** (**quelqu'un/quelque chose**).

il n'y a qu'une solution: ça doit être la batterie there's only one explanation: it must be the battery. **Ne…que** means 'only'.

je ne vois que ça that's all I can think of (literally I see only that).

ce que je peux te proposer what I suggest (literally that which I can suggest to you).

je vais chercher ma voiture I'll go and get my car. **Chercher** is 'to look for', but **aller chercher** is 'to go and get'.

On essaie de relancer la batterie We'll try to jump-start the battery.

il faut que tu roules you must drive around.

je te conseille d'aller directement chez un garagiste I advise you to go directly to a garage. **Un garagiste** is actually a person who runs a garage.

4 By a process of elimination, work out which of the captions in the box is appropriate for each of the problems illustrated and then write under the drawing to help you commit the vocabulary to memory. You can check specific words in the vocabulary at the back of the book if you need to do so.

> **Les toilettes sont bloquées.**
>
> **Le tuyau de la machine à laver est bouché.**
>
> **Ma voiture ne démarre pas.**
>
> **Le chauffage central ne marche pas.**
>
> **L'ampoule a sauté.**
>
> **Je suis en panne d'essence.**

Answers p. 144

5 On the recording for this exercise, there are four snippets of conversation between a holidaymaker and the woman from whom he is renting a **gîte**. It is fortunate she lives next door to it, because a number of things in the house go wrong. As well as the vocabulary from Exercise 4, you will need to understand:

allumer	to switch on
le chauffe-eau	water-heater
le fusible	fuse
jeter	to throw (in)
boucher	to block

Listen to the exchanges and, for each one, see if you can note down:

	What the problem is...	What the landlady says she will do...
Exchange (a):	_____	_____
	_____	_____
	_____	_____
Exchange (b):	_____	i. _____
	_____	_____
	_____	
	_____	and, if that fails:
	_____	ii. _____
	_____	_____
	_____	_____
	_____	_____
Exchange (c):	_____	_____
	_____	_____
	_____	_____
Exchange (d):	_____	_____
	_____	_____
	_____	_____

Answers p. 144

6 Your car won't start and you ask a stranger to help you. You will need to recycle phrases from Conversations 1 and 2.

Matthieu has lost his bag

Réceptionniste	Bonjour!
Matthieu	Bonjour! Excusez-moi…Je suis allé en ville cette après-midi et je suis parti avec ma, ma sacoche et j'ai perdu ma sacoche en ville dans un magasin…je me rappelle plus le, le magasin et…j'avais dedans tous mes papiers, ma carte d'identité…mon permis de conduire, ma carte grise, tous mes, tous les papiers importants dont j'ai besoin pour le voyage et…il faudrait que vous m'aidiez pour que je puisse les retrouver.
Réceptionniste	Vous n'avez vraiment aucune idée de l'endroit où vous avez pu les perdre?
(Matthieu	Aucune idée. Je ne me rappelle plus du tout.)
Réceptionniste	OK. Je vais prendre votre nom…
Matthieu	Oui…
Réceptionniste	Alors, vous êtes Monsieur…
Matthieu	Monsieur Pouget.
Réceptionniste	P-O-U…
Matthieu	G-E-T.
Réceptionniste	G-E-T. Votre prénom?
Matthieu	Matthieu: M-A-deux T-H-I-E-U.
Réceptionniste	Voilà. Et je vais appeler la gendarmerie: peut-être que quelqu'un les aurait trouvés et les aurait déposés. (*She telephones.*) Oui, bonjour! C'est l'hôtel Comfort Inn à Ramonville. Je vous appelle puisque…un de mes clients a perdu ses papiers dans un magasin du centre-ville de Toulouse – il ne sait plus du tout lequel – et j'aimerais savoir si, par hasard, on ne vous les aurait pas déposés…Donc, ce sont des papiers – passeport, permis de conduire…tous ses papiers d'identité…au nom de Pouget: P-O-U-G-E-T, Matthieu: M-A-deux T-H-I-E-U…Oui? C'est vrai? On vous les a déposés?…OK, bon, ben, je transmets tout de suite la bonne nouvelle à mon client et il passe les récupérer, ben, immédiatement…Merci beaucoup. Au revoir.

VOCABULARY

dedans	inside
par hasard	by (any) chance
transmettre	to convey, to transmit
la nouvelle	news
récupérer	to recover, to collect
passer	to pass, to come over

j'ai perdu ma sacoche I have lost my bag.
Une sacoche is the kind of handbag which many French men carry; a woman's handbag is **un sac à main**. While you are about it, learn **un portefeuille** 'a wallet'.

je (ne) me rappelle plus le magasin I don't remember the shop any more. From the reflexive verb **se rappeler**. **Ne…plus** means 'no more', though, as with other negatives, the **ne** is often omitted in speech.

mon permis de conduire, ma carte grise
my driving licence, my vehicle registration document.

tous les papiers importants dont j'ai besoin pour le voyage all the important papers which I need for the journey (literally of which I have need for the journey). For **dont**, see the Grammar section.

il faudrait que vous m'aidiez pour que je puisse les retrouver I need your help to find them (literally it would be necessary that you should help me in order that I may find them again). This is grammatically complicated, with a conditional (**il faudrait**) followed by two subjunctives…don't worry about it!

l'endroit où vous avez pu les perdre the place where you may have lost them (literally the place where you have been able them to lose).

peut-être que quelqu'un les aurait trouvés et les aurait déposés perhaps someone may have found them and handed them in. **Aurait** is in the conditional, indicating that this is by no means certain. For an explanation of the **-s** on **trouvés** and **déposés**, see the note at the end of p. 14.

Ramonville a suburb of Toulouse.

lequel which (referring to a masculine singular noun). You met **laquelle** in Conversation 2. The plurals are **lesquels** and **lesquelles**.

on ne vous les aurait pas déposés somebody hasn't handed them in to you. For the word order of pronouns like **vous** and **les**, see Grammar.

French children enjoy chanting:

Quand un gendarme rit dans la gendarmerie, tous les gendarmes rient dans la gendarmerie.

rire to laugh

PRACTICE

7
Test yourself to see whether you can say all the letters of the alphabet in French, then listen to Jean-Pierre saying them on the recording. If you are not very confident at spelling in French, this is your opportunity to work at it. As well as reciting the alphabet, it is useful to practise spelling your name and your address and perhaps the number of your car.

8
You are at the police station, reporting your own lost bag. You will hear the verb **voler** 'to steal'. (It also means to 'fly'.)

9 With all the talk of problems in this unit, it seems a good idea to think about insurance. Here are details of the cancellation insurance offered in a travel brochure. Try not to be fazed by the legal jargon – just see if you can understand enough of it to answer the questions at the end.

ASSURANCE

L'assurance annulation prend en charge les frais prévus ci-dessus, dans les cas suivants:

— Accident, maladie ou décès de l'assuré, de son conjoint ou concubin, des ascendants, descendants, des frères, sœurs, beaux-frères, belles-sœurs, gendres et brus, à l'exclusion des maladies connues lors de l'inscription.

— Préjudices graves nécessitant la présence de l'assuré le jour du départ, dûs à un vol, à un incendie ou à des éléments naturels et atteignant les locaux professionnels ou privés.

— Licenciement économique de l'assuré. [Redundancy]

— Grossesse. [Pregnancy]

For which of the following could you claim?

a Illness of your partner

b Accident happening to your brother-in-law

c Death of your sister-in-law from a long-term illness

d A burglary at your office

e A fire in your house

f Redundancy of your partner

Answers p. 144

g Pregnancy of your cat

KEY WORDS AND PHRASES

pourriez-vous m'aider?	could you help me?
j'ai besoin d'aide	I need help
au secours!	help!
faire le plein d'essence	to fill it up with petrol
le carburant	fuel
l'essence (f.)	(two-star) petrol
le super	four-star/super petrol
sans plomb	unleaded
c'est très gentil/aimable	that's very kind
qu'est-ce qui vous arrive?	what's the problem?
que se passe-t-il?	what's the matter?
la machine n'accepte pas ma carte	the machine won't accept my card
les cartes britanniques n'ont pas de puce	British cards have no micro-chip
on doit mettre un code	you have to tap in a PIN-number
c'est fête	it's a (bank) holiday
j'ai de l'argent en espèces/ en liquide	I have money in cash
est-ce que vous voudriez bien mettre votre carte à vous?	would you be willing to put in *your* card?
des câbles de démarrage	jump-leads
relancer la batterie	to jump-start the battery
recharger la batterie	to recharge the battery
au moins	at least
ça ne marche pas	it doesn't work
ma voiture ne démarre pas	my car won't start
ma voiture est en panne	my car has broken down
être en panne d'essence	to have run out of petrol
ça doit être la batterie	it must be the battery
je te propose	I suggest (to you)
je te conseille d'aller chez un garagiste	I advise you to go to a garage
j'ai perdu ma sacoche	I have lost my bag
le papier	paper
tous mes papiers	all my papers
le permis de conduire	driving licence
la carte grise	vehicle registration document
la gendarmerie	police station
par hasard	by (any) chance
transmettre	to convey, to transmit
la nouvelle	news
récupérer	to recover, to collect
je (ne) me rappelle plus le magasin	I don't remember any more the shop
l'endroit (m.)	the place

12

Write a reply to each of these questions on the model:

Est-ce que tu feras la vaisselle? / Oui, je la ferai!

a   Est-ce que tu prendras ta sacoche? _____

b   Est-ce que tu cherches tes papiers? _____

c   Est-ce que tu as trouvé ton passeport? _____

d   Est-ce que tu as ta carte grise? _____

e   Est-ce que tu changeras ton dernier chèque de voyage?

_____

f   Est-ce que tu penseras à prendre tes clés? [Careful – you are taking your keys, not thinking your keys, so **prendre** is the relevant verb.]

_____

Answers p. 144

Order of pronouns

On <u>vous les</u> a déposés?
On ne <u>vous les</u> aurait pas déposés.

If you need to use **me**, **te**, **nous** or **vous** in the same sentence as **le**, **la** or **les**, then the **me**, **te**, **nous** or **vous** comes first. More examples:

Je <u>te le</u> donne.	I am giving it to you.
Elle <u>me l'</u>a dit.	She told me so (literally She has told me it).
Il <u>nous la</u> confie.	He entrusts it/her to us.

13

Put the French words into the right order to make them mean the same as the English:

a   nous   donnes   tu   la _____
You give it to us.

b   le   je   confie   te _____
I entrust it to you.

c   l'   vous   ai   je   dit _____
I told you so.

d   les   me   on   volés   a _____
Someone has stolen them from me.

Answers p. 144

Dont

Les papiers dont j'ai besoin
The papers I need
(literally The papers of which I have need)

Un auteur dont j'ai oublié le nom
An author whose name I have forgotten
(literally An author of whom I have forgotten the name)

L'ami dont je t'ai parlé
The friend I have told you about
(literally The friend of whom I to you have spoken)

For the moment, it is enough to understand **dont** when you meet it.

Unit 9   No problem!

14 **Pile ou face?** Heads or tails? – well, actually tails or heads, since it is that way round in the French. You don't need a dice to play – just a coin to toss. For heads, you move on one square (**une case**), for tails two. Each time you land on a square with something written on it, your partner (if you have one) reads it out. You then recap on what you have to do, changing the **vous** forms and instructions into sentences with **je**. E.g. If your partner reads out **Votre voiture ne démarre pas: passez un tour** 'miss a go', you say **Ma voiture ne démarre pas: je dois passer un tour.**

Point de départ

1

2

3 Vous avez trouvé 150 euros dans la rue: allez à la gendarmerie.

Votre voiture ne démarre pas: passez un tour.

4 Vous avez oublié votre portefeuille: retournez au point de départ.

Gendarmerie

7 Un gendarme veut voir vos papiers: retournez à la gendarmerie.

6 Gendarmerie.

5 La route est bonne: avancez à la case 9

8 Vous avez reçu un chèque: allez à la banque.

9 Vous avez trop bu donc vous ne pouvez pas conduire: passez un tour.

10 Station-service.

11 Il faut recharger votre batterie: passez un tour.

12 Vous prenez un taxi: allez à la banque.

15 La machine n'accepte pas votre carte: passez un tour.

16 Quelqu'un vous aide: avancez à la case 18.

14 Banque.

13 Vous avez perdu votre sacoche: allez à la gendarmerie.

17 Vous êtes en panne d'essence: retournez à la station-service.

18 Vous êtes presque arrivé(e) – mais faites attention aux voleurs!

19 On vous a volé votre argent: retournez à la banque.

20 ARRIVÉE

ANSWERS P. 144

EXERCISE 1

(a) Yes (b) No (c) Yes (d) No (Visa) (e) No
(f) Yes

EXERCISE 3

(a) les petites et moyennes banques (b) n'oubliez pas (c) pratiquemment partout (d) une telle distance (e) les chambres et tables d'hôtes (f) il est difficile de les changer (g) on peut tirer du liquide (h) des/les chèques en bois

EXERCISE 4

(a) Ma voiture ne démarre pas. (b) Je suis en panne d'essence. (c) L'ampoule a sauté. (d) Les toilettes sont bloquées. (e) Le chauffage central ne marche pas. (f) Le tuyau de la machine à laver est bouché.

EXERCISE 5

Exchange (a): No hot water in the house / Come and switch on the water-heater. Exchange (b): Electricity not working / i. Come and see if a fuse has blown ii. Call an electrician. Exchange (c): Three bulbs have blown / Buy some (while she is shopping in town this afternoon). Exchange (d): The toilet is blocked / Call a plumber (and tell him it is urgent).

EXERCISE 9

(a) (b) (d) (e)

EXERCISE 10

(a) Je n'ai pas de carte. (b) Elle n'a pas d'amis.
(c) Ils n'ont pas de voiture. (d) Il ne veut pas de gâteau. (e) On n'achète pas de viande.
(f) Tu ne bois pas de whisky.

EXERCISE 11

(a) Elle t'aime. (b) Il nous donnera l'argent.
(c) Il me comprend. (d) Nous vous écoutons.
(e) Ils nous conseillent d'aller à la banque.
(f) Je te parle!

EXERCISE 12

(a) Oui, je la prendrai! (b) Oui, je les cherche!
(c) Oui, je l'ai trouvé! (d) Oui, je l'ai! (e) Oui, je le changerai! (f) Oui, je penserai à les prendre!

EXERCISE 13

(a) Tu nous la donnes. (b) Je te le confie.
(c) Je vous l'ai dit. (d) On me les a volés.

EXERCISE 14

2. Ma voiture ne démarre pas: je dois passer un tour.
3. J'ai trouvé 150 euros dans la rue: je dois aller à la gendarmerie.
4. J'ai oublié mon portefeuille: je dois retourner au point de départ.
5. La route est bonne: je dois/peux avancer à la case 9.
7. Un gendarme veut voir mes papiers: je dois retourner à la gendarmerie.
8. J'ai reçu un chèque: je dois aller à la banque.
9. J'ai trop bu donc je ne peux pas conduire: je dois passer un tour.
11. Il faut recharger ma batterie: je dois passer un tour.
12. Je prends un taxi: je dois aller à la banque.
13. J'ai perdu ma sacoche: je dois aller à la gendarmerie.
15. La machine n'accepte pas ma carte: je dois passer un tour.
16. Quelqu'un m'aide: je dois/peux avancer à la case 18.
17. Je suis en panne d'essence: je dois retourner à la station-service.
18. Je suis presque arrivé(e) – mais je dois faire attention aux voleurs!
19. On m'a volé mon argent: je dois retourner à la banque.
20. Je suis arrivé(e)!

10 TOULOUSE

WHAT YOU WILL LEARN

▶ something about Toulouse
▶ describing the attractions of a town
▶ discussing what it is like to live in a particular place
▶ something about the Canal du Midi
▶ talking about waterways and leisure

POINTS TO REMEMBER

Do you remember how the conditional works?
As an example, for the verb **être** it is: **je serais** 'I would be', **tu serais, il/elle serait, nous serions, vous seriez, ils/elles seraient**.
If you are a bit hazy about it, this would be a good moment to look back at Unit 7.

BEFORE YOU BEGIN

Listening to the Conversations in this unit will stretch your comprehension, for different reasons:

■ in Conversation 1 the guide's speech is very fluent and rapid
■ in Conversation 2, the friends speak unfluently and colloquially and interrupt each other
■ in Conversation 3, Bruno gives a great deal of information in his warm Toulousain accent

These are all styles of speech you will meet in France, so it is good to get some practice in advance.

The centre of Toulouse

The historical monuments of Toulouse

Guide

Toulouse est une ville très riche sur le plan du patrimoine. Nous avons, au cœur de la cité, plusieurs édifices remarquables, en particulier le Capitole, qui est

notre hôtel de ville, qui a été construit dès l'époque de la Renaissance et terminé au dix-neuvième siècle. Nous avons également la basilique Saint-Sernin, qui est un édifice roman, construit entre le onzième et le quinzième siècle, un centre de pèlerinage, un centre de dévotion. Nous avons aussi le couvent des Jacobins, qui est un édifice gothique, construit entre le treizième et le quatorzième siècle par l'ordre des Dominicains, et qui constitue la maison-mère de cette communauté. Mais nous avons aussi la période de Renaissance, qui est très riche, avec des hôtels particuliers qui sont remarquables: l'hôtel de Jean de Bernuy, l'hôtel de Pierre d'Assézat, contemporains des réalisations de François 1er et d'Henri II.

VOCABULARY	
le patrimoine	heritage
le cœur	heart
l'édifice (m.)	edifice, building
terminer	to complete
le siècle	century
la basilique	basilica
construit	built
le pèlerinage	pilgrimage
gothique	Gothic
la maison-mère	mother-house
la communauté	community
contemporain	contemporary
la réalisation	creation

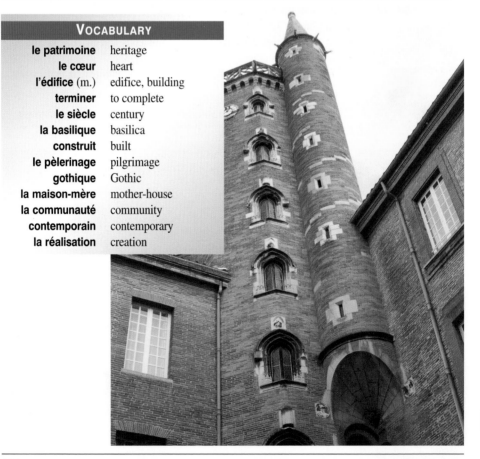

dès l'époque de la Renaissance from the time of the Renaissance onwards.

roman Romanesque (what we call Norman). Roman is **romain**.

le couvent religious house, which can be a convent, a monastery or, as here, a priory.

par l'ordre des Dominicains by the Dominican Order.

des hôtels particuliers private mansions. This second meaning of the word **hôtel** often catches foreigners out.

de François 1ᵉʳ et d'Henri II of these two Kings of France. Note that 'the first' is **Premier** (with no **le**) but that subsequent monarchs are **Deux, Trois, Quatre**, etc. It is the same pattern as for dates **(le premier mars, le deux mars, le trois mars**, etc.).

Les Jacobins

PRACTICE

1 In the unscripted recording made on location for this exercise, Yves also talks about Toulouse. Listen and see if you can answer the questions.

a Around what date do the students leave Toulouse? _____

b What is usually the maximum length of stay for tourists who come in the summer? _____

c Why don't they stay longer than that?

_____

d What does Yves say they visit?

i. _____

ii. _____

e What is the town like in August?

Answers p. 160

_____

4

In another authentic recording, Alain contrasts Toulouse and Paris. In what order does he make the following points? Number them in the boxes.

a 500 euros rents a bed-sit in Paris or a four-roomed flat in Toulouse. ☐

b I am frustrated by the importance of Paris. ☐

c I couldn't live in Paris. ☐

d A cup of coffee in Toulouse costs 1.50€ – in Paris it is 2.50€. ☐

e Paris is the capital. ☐

f Life is expensive in Paris. ☐

g Everything happens in Paris. ☐

Answers p. 160 **h** The problem is that Paris moves faster than its inhabitants. ☐

5

Follow Philippe's prompts as Marianne asks you how you like Toulouse.

6   More information about Toulouse, again taken from a tourist brochure:

Toulouse, ville de culture, cité du futur

Toulouse aime la nuit. Il faut dire que la ville a su préserver, comme au temps des troubadours, son penchant naturel pour les spectacles: le Capitole reste un haut lieu de l'art lyrique, les caves-poésie perpétuent la culture occitane, le théâtre Daniel Sorano, les cafés-théâtre, les concerts de la Halle aux Grains, proposent des créations originales réputées. Enfin 'Musique d'été', organisé par l'Office de Tourisme, et le festival 'Piano Jacobins' remportent chaque année un énorme succès (juillet à septembre).

Toulouse, ville ouverte sur l'avenir, est également fière de son profil dans bon nombre de domaines scientifiques: aéronautique, espace, électronique, informatique, automatisme, électrochimie, biologie, agronomie, médecine vétérinaire, médecine…Neuf mille chercheurs consacrent leur talent à faire de Toulouse un centre de 'vocations' modernes et de rencontres scientifiques et techniques au plus haut niveau.

VOCABULARY

le haut lieu	major centre (literally a high place)
le chercheur	researcher

True or false?

a   The Tourist Office organises a summer music festival. ☐ ☐

b   Concerts are held in the old cornmarket. ☐ ☐

c   There are just 900 researchers in Toulouse. ☐ ☐

d   Le Capitole is a major venue for vocal music. ☐ ☐

e   Information technology is one of the city's specialities. ☐ ☐

f   The piano festival in les Jacobins takes place in the winter. ☐ ☐

Answers p. 160   **g**   There are cellars where you can hear Occitan poetry recitals. ☐ ☐

Le label UNESCO sur la bonne voie

Avis favorable: c'est le verdict des experts mandatés pour le classement du canal du Midi au patrimoine mondial des grands sites et monuments. La décision sera prise le 7 décembre à Mexico.

C'est dans les premiers jours de décembre que l'UNESCO dira si le canal du Midi mérite d'être inscrit parmi les grands sites du patrimoine mondial.

Une sorte de 'top planétaire' des plus beaux monuments et sites du globe, dans lequel figurent notamment le Mont-Saint-Michel, le Taj Mahal ou la muraille de Chine. Les 21 membres de la commission des sites (sur 147 états que compte l'UNESCO) doivent se réunir du 5 au 7 décembre à Mexico, notamment pour statuer sur la demande d'inscription de 33 sites de par le monde, dont le canal du Midi.

VOCABULARY	
le top	top of the charts
statuer	to give a ruling

a How many states belong to UNESCO? _____

b How many new candidates are there for inclusion in the list of the world's major heritage sites? _____

c When will the commission be meeting to judge the applications?
_____

d Which three sites are mentioned as already having the status of world heritage sites? _____
_____

e Find in the text the French for:

to meet _____

notably _____

world(-wide) _____

Answers p. 160   planetary _____

KEY WORDS AND PHRASES

le patrimoine	heritage
le cœur	heart
un édifice roman/gothique	a Romanesque/Gothic building
terminer	to complete
la basilique	basilica
l'hôtel particulier	private mansion
construit au quinzième siècle	built in the fifteenth century
le pèlerinage	pilgrimage
la communauté	community
contemporain	contemporary
la réalisation	creation
à dimensions humaines	to human dimensions
le climat	climate
l'activité culturelle	cultural activity
tout à fait	exactly
un endroit où il est agréable	a place where it is pleasant
de travailler et de vivre,	to work and to live,
c'est-à-dire	that is to say
d'avoir des loisirs	to spend one's leisure
posséder	to possess
bouger	to move
contrairement à	unlike
la mer me manque	I miss the sea
le canal	canal
dans cette direction,	in this direction
ça va vers Sète	it goes towards Sète
la plaisance	pleasure (cruising)
la péniche	barge
ç'a été construit	it was built
au moment de Louis XIV	at the time of Louis XIV
ç'a permis tout un	it made possible a whole
développement économique	economic development
de la région,	of the region,
parce qu'on pouvait	because one could
transporter des marchandises	transport goods
pour pas cher	cheaply
actuellement	nowadays
on transporte le blé	they transport corn
le ciment	cement
le charbon	coal
dépasser	to exceed
on peut faire du cyclisme	you can go cycling
on peut courir	you can run
ça m'est arrivé plusieurs fois	it has happened to me several times
l'arbre (m.)	tree
c'est très frais/ombragé	it's very cool/shady
la rive	bank
se promener	to go for a walk
se promener à cheval	to go horse-riding

Qu'est-ce qui?

You won't need it anything like as often as **qui?** and **que?**, but 'what?' as the subject of a verb is **qu'est-ce <u>qui</u>?**:

Qu'est-ce qui fait ce bruit?   What's making that noise?

Qu'est-ce qui compte le plus?   What matters most?

Quoi?

'What?' after a preposition is **quoi?**:

Tu le fais avec quoi?   What are you making it with?

De quoi parlez-vous?   What are you talking about?

12   Write **qu'est-ce qui**, **qu'est-ce que** or **quoi** in each of the gaps:

a   _____tu as dit?

b   _____arrive?

c   A _____penses-tu?

d   _____est le plus important dans la vie?

e   _____vous avez l'intention de faire?

f   En _____consiste ce projet?

Answers p. 160

You will find that the use of
> **qui?** and **que?**
> **qui** and **que**
> **qu'est-ce qui?** and **qu'est-ce que?**
> and **quoi?**

falls into place with practice.

13 This letter was sent out by a boat-hire company. You will probably recognise most of the words in it, apart from

la foule	crowd
s'étonner	to astonish oneself
la pêche	fishing
le chemin de halage	towpath

NICOLS

Location de vedettes fluviales sur les plus belles voies navigables
Route du Puy-Saint-Bonnet - 49300 CHOLET - Tél: 02.41.56.46.56 -
Fax 02.41.56.46.47
Internet: http://www.nicols.com

Ref:nv

Cholet, le 15/06/2003

Monsieur, Madame,

Le tourisme fluvial?

C'est le moyen idéal de passer de vraies vacances, au calme, loin de la foule.

Plongez dans un univers de plénitude, goûtez aux plaisirs de redécouvrir la vraie nature, partagez un moment de bonheur avec votre famille, vos amis... Etonnez-vous en devenant capitaine confirmé après une simple initiation à la navigation. Savourez les parties de pêche, balades à bicyclette sur les chemins de halage, découvertes du patrimoine, baignades et après-midi de détente au soleil...

Vous rêvez déjà à vos prochaines vacances sur l'eau?

Contactez-nous ! Nous nous ferons un plaisir de vous aider à choisir le bateau idéal pour cette croisière sur une de nos dix-huit bases, en France, en Allemagne ou en Hollande.

A très bientôt !

Votre Centrale de Réservation

a Drawing on the language of the letter, the Conversations and the recording for Exercise 8, write five sentences vaunting the merits of a boating holiday on the canal going through Toulouse. Mention some of the attractions of the town as well as those of the waterway. Some of your sentences could begin

J'aime...	J'aimerais ...
On peut...	On pourrait...
Il y a...	Il y aurait...
C'est très agréable de...	Ce serait très agréable de...
(+ infinitive)	(+ infinitive)

b If you are working with a partner, compare what you have written and and cross off any sentences or phrases which you both have. Then repeat the exercise and see if you can build up the number of sentences which are not crossed off. When you have finished, you can compare your sentences with the ones Marianne produces on the recording.

The future of work

Roger

Que nous réserve l'avenir au niveau de la vie pratique de chacun? C'est une, c'est une grande question. Personnellement, je crois que…vouloir tout ramener à des questions de rendement financier– c'est, bien entendu, indispensable, la finance – mais, ça ne suffit pas.

Il y a le problème en particulier du chômage. Il est certain que, en 2005, il y aura, en France, environ 24 millions de personnes susceptibles de travailler. Et, dans l'état actuel de l'économie, il y aura 19 millions d'emplois, ce qui voudrait dire qu'il y aurait cinq millions de chômeurs. Donc, plutôt que d'emplois, il faut parler de travail, et voir comment répartir ce travail…Pour des personnes âgées, ça va, mais pour des jeunes aujourd'hui, c'est vraiment inquiétant.

VOCABULARY

bien entendu	of course
le chômage	unemployment
le chômeur	unemployed person
environ	around, approximately
répartir	share out
inquiétant	worrying

Que nous réserve l'avenir au niveau de la vie pratique de chacun? What does the future have in store for us at the level of each person's practical life? A less polished speaker would have said **Qu'est-ce que l'avenir nous réserve au niveau pratique?**

vouloir tout ramener à des questions de rendement financier to want to reduce everything (literally to bring everything back) to questions of financial return.

ça ne suffit pas it's not enough (literally that does not suffice). You will often hear **Ça suffit!** as an attempt to quell a naughty child.

susceptibles de travailler capable of working/eligible to work. **Susceptible** on its own means 'oversensitive' or 'touchy', but **susceptible de** is used to express potential: **ce poste est susceptible de m'intéresser** 'this job might interest me'; **cet article est susceptible de plusieurs**

interprétations 'this article is open to several interpretations'.

dans l'état actuel de l'économie in the present state of the economy.

ce qui voudrait dire qu'… (that) which would mean that… This is from **vouloir dire** 'to mean' (literally to want to say). Learn also: **je veux dire** 'I mean'; **qu'est-ce que ça veut dire?** 'what does that mean?' **qu'est-ce que vous voulez dire?** 'what do you mean?'

plutôt que d'emplois, il faut parler de travail Rather than (speaking) of jobs, we should speak of work.

1 This text is taken from an article by Gérard Adam in the newspaper *La Croix* on the theme of 'lies, damned lies and statistics'. See what you make of it!

Chômage: un indice contestable

Le nombre des demandeurs d'emploi publié chaque mois par le ministère du travail et habituellement retenue par les médias – 3 112 800 en septembre – ne correspond pas à la réalité du chômage. Ce chiffre ne représente que les personnes qui recherchent un contrat à durée indéterminée et à plein temps.

Cependant, de plus en plus, se développent le temps partiel et les contrats à durée déterminée. Aussi de nombreux chômeurs sont-ils demandeurs de ce type d'emploi (par exemple, dans les domaines saisonniers de l'agriculture ou du tourisme).

Au total, il faudrait ajouter environ 750 000 personnes pour avoir une mesure plus exacte du chômage.

VOCABULARY

le chiffre	figure
cependant	however

What is the French for the following?

a the reality of unemployment

_____

b fixed-term contracts

_____

c seasonal areas

_____

d the number of jobseekers

_____

e full-time

à _____

f part-time (work)

le _____

g to add

_____

h approximately

Answers p. 176

_____

See if you can use some of that vocabulary to write or say out loud a few sentences about your own (un)employment situation. Another phrase you might need is **à la retraite** 'retired'.

Mais c'est ce que le maire compte faire pour l'avenir! But that's what the mayor intends to do for the future! **Compter faire** is literally 'to reckon to do':
Qu'est-ce que tu comptes faire? What are you intending to do?

Les utilisateurs de voiture râlent quand même Car-users moan anyway.

comment on va faire pour se garer? how are we going to park? Another example of the reflexive verb **se garer**:

Vous ne pouvez pas vous garer ici! You can't park here!

sans payer en plus le transport en commun without paying in addition for public transport. In Unit 6, you met a similarly constructed phrase:
sans consommer d'énergie without consuming any energy:
sans + infinitive without + -ing

ça sera difficile de satisfaire tout le monde it will be difficult to satisfy everybody.

PRACTICE

4 On the recording, Jean-Pierre and Marianne talk about solutions to city-centre congestion.
Who says…?

		Jean-Pierre	Marianne
a	The new buses are easier of access for the elderly.	☐	☐
b	Cycle paths are being opened this year.	☐	☐
c	They are going to build a new line for the metro.	☐	☐
d	If they build a good cycle network, I'll happily leave my car at home.	☐	☐
e	The traffic here is becoming hellish.	☐	☐
f	I read about the cycle tracks in the newspaper.	☐	☐

Answers p. 176

VOCABULARY

infernal	hellish
la circulation	traffic
la piste cyclable	cycle track
ridicule	ridiculous
à la limite	you could even say (literally at the limit)
interdire	to forbid, to ban
la ligne	line
accessible	accessible
tant mieux!	so much the better!

learn also:

tant pis!	too bad! (the **-s** is not pronounced)

5 Your chance to join in the debate. You have just arrived late for lunch with Marianne…

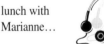

6 This article describes measures being taken to reduce the number of cars in one city centre.

CÔTÉ PARKINGS

De nouvelles dispositions tarifaires sont entrées en vigueur le 7 octobre. Désormais, dans les parkings de l'hyper-centre, le paiement se fait à la demi-heure (1 euro la demi-heure jusqu'à deux heures de stationnement, et tarif à l'heure au-delà). Dans les autres parkings, le tarif baisse à 1 euro de l'heure.

Ces mesures ont été décidées en concertation entre les associations de commerçants, la Chambre de commerce et d'industrie et les sociétés exploitant les parkings.

VOCABULARY	
entrer en vigueur	to come into effect
désormais	from now on
baisser	to lower, to become lower

a How much does it cost to park for an hour

　i. in a car-park in the very centre of town?

　_____

　ii. in an ordinary car-park?

　_____

b Which organisation collaborated with the firms running the car parks and the traders' associations to fix the new parking tariffs?

_____

c When did the new regulations come into force?

_____

d What colloquial expression is used in the text for 'the very centre'?

Answers p. 176

_____

CONVERSATION 3

 Censorship

Anne	Moi, j'ai été scandalisée par l'arrêt d'une émission satirique suite à un sketch particulier où on voyait des acteurs	

LISTEN FOR...

l'arrêt d'une émission satirique	stopping of a satirical programme
tuer les hommes politiques actuels	to kill the current politicians
au moyen de truquage	by means of special effects

en train de tuer les hommes politiques actuels, au moyen de truquage, bien évidemment.

Pierre Je suis d'accord, mais…il faut pas que, que sous prétexte de l'insolence et de la satire, on, on se permette des choses qui, qui amènent trop loin, trop loin les gens qui regardent cette émission et qui peuvent donner des idées négatives.

Anne Oui, mais, à ton avis, est-ce que vraiment toutes les personnes qui regardent l'émission vont être incitées comme ça à la violence, au meurtre? C'est des personnes, c'est vraiment des, des personnes très particulières, déséquilibrées, à la base.

Pierre Non, je ne dis pas qu'elles seraient incitées, par ces, par ces images, mais elles n'ont pas les moyens de, souvent de faire la part des choses entre ce qui est la fiction et ce qui est la réalité et c'est vrai que ça paraît tellement simple d'un seul coup de pouvoir tuer qui on veut comme on veut.

VOCABULARY

scandalisé(e)	scandalised, shocked
suite à	following
évidemment	obviously
sous prétexte de	under pretext of
négatif, -ive	negative
inciter	to incite
le meurtre	murder
déséquilibré(e)	unbalanced
d'un seul coup	at a stroke

des acteurs en train de tuer actors in the process of killing. A further example: **Je suis en train d'écrire à mon frère** 'I am (in the process of) writing to my brother (at this very moment).'

il faut pas que…on se permette one must not permit oneself. **Permette** is from the subjunctive of the verb **permettre**.

des choses qui amènent trop loin les gens qui regardent cette émission things which lead on too far the people who watch the broadcast.

qu'elles seraient incitées that they would be incited. **Elles** refers to **personnes**, which is a feminine word.

elles n'ont pas les moyens they are not able. **Les moyens** = 'the means'. Learn also the adjective **moyen(ne)** 'average', 'middling'. **La moyenne** is 'the mean' (in statistics) and is also used for the pass-mark in an exam.

de faire la part des choses entre ce qui est la fiction et ce qui est la réalité to make a distinction between what is fiction and what is reality.

de pouvoir tuer qui on veut comme on veut to be able to kill whom you want as you want.

7

It can be helpful to spend time practising the pronunciation of a few words carefully chosen to illustrate general points. On the recording, Jean-Pierre says some words and phrases taken from the Conversation. Repeat them after him, bearing the following pointers in mind:

j'ai été scandalisée – be careful not to put a [y] after any of the [é] sounds – and remember that the '**an**' is a nasal vowel, so the '**n**' is not pronounced separately.

évidemment – the '**emm**' is pronounced [**amm**] and the '**ent**' is the same vowel as the '**an**' in **scandalisée**.

je suis d'accord – the [**or**] is pronounced further back in the mouth than the English [or].

à ton avis – as with [é], be careful not to add a [y] at the end of **avis**. Because **ton** is followed by a vowel, it ceases to be a nasal and the '**n**' is pronounced.

vraiment – gives practice at the French [**r**].

ça paraît tellement simple – another [**r**] and a different nasal vowel in **simple**.

des personnes déséquilibrées – two more [**r**] sounds – and **déséquilibrées** is quite a tongue-twister!

8

Indicate your reaction to each of the statements on this opinion poll.

A VOTRE AVIS...

■ Il y a trop de violence à la télévision.
  D'accord / Pas d'accord / Je ne sais pas

■ Voir des actes de violence à la télévision peut inciter les gens à les imiter.
  D'accord / Pas d'accord / Je ne sais pas

■ Puisque les enfants sont particulièrement susceptibles d'être influencés, les émissions montrant des actes de violence ne doivent pas être programmées avant 21 h.
  D'accord / Pas d'accord / Je ne sais pas

■ Il y a trop de sexe à la télévision.
  D'accord / Pas d'accord / Je ne sais pas

■ Il n'y a pas assez de sexe à la télévision.
  D'accord / Pas d'accord / Je ne sais pas

9 On the recording, you can eavesdrop on an argument about pornographic magazines. See if you can number the following points in the order in which you hear them in this conversation.

a In a democracy, you have to respect market forces. ☐

b I pity (**je plains**, from the verb **plaindre**) the wives and children of men who buy porno magazines. ☐

c I am disgusted by porno magazines. They shouldn't be allowed. ☐

d I don't buy porno magazines, but I know men who do – they need them. ☐

e Some of the buyers are good family-men. ☐

f That doesn't mean pornographic magazines are a good thing. These pictures degrade women. ☐

g You're a man, so of course you like pictures of naked women ready to do anything. ☐

h There are buyers for these magazines. ☐

i People only buy them because they exist. They could do without, unless they are really unhinged. ☐

Answers p. 176

le vingt-et-unième siècle	twenty-first century
que nous réserve l'avenir (m.)	what does the future hold in store
au niveau de la vie pratique?	for us at the level of practical life?
c'est une grande question	that's a big question
religieux, -euse	religious
le rendement financier	financial return
personnellement, je crois que	personally, I believe that
ça ne suffit pas	that's not enough
dans l'état actuel	in the present state
de l'économie	of the economy
il y a le problème	there is the problem
du chômage	of unemployment
le chômeur	unemployed person
comment répartir le travail	how to share out work
pour des personnes âgées,	for elderly people,
ça va,	it's all right,
mais pour des jeunes	but for young people
c'est vraiment inquiétant	it's really worrying
je veux dire	I mean
qu'est-ce que ça veut dire?	what does that mean?
qu'est-ce que vous voulez dire?	what do you mean?
excuse(z)-moi	forgive me
je suis désolée pour le retard	I am very sorry to be late
il y avait des embouteillages	there were traffic jams
des centres-villes piétons	pedestrianised town centres
le transport en commun	public transport
comment on va faire	how are we going
pour se garer?	to park?
bien entendu	of course
évidemment	obviously
en fait	actually
interdire l'accès (m.)	to forbid access
l'émission (f.) satirique	satirical programme
des acteurs en train de tuer	actors in the process of killing
les hommes politiques actuels	the current politicians
au moyen de truquage	by means of special effects
scandalisé(e)	scandalised, shocked
suite à	following
sous prétexte de	under pretext of
inciter au meurtre	to incite to murder
déséquilibré(e)	unbalanced
d'un seul coup	at a stroke
les droits de l'homme	human rights
avoir le droit de parler	to have the right to speak

The words and phrases on p. 175 are also key language for this unit.

Stating your opinion

There is little that is new on this page: it pulls together and consolidates expressions you have already met, adding one or two more for completeness.

12 Can you translate into English the following ways of stating your opinion?

a   à mon avis...   _____

b   personnellement...   _____

c   je pense que...   _____

d   je crois que...   _____

e   je sais que...   _____

f   il est certain que... _____

g   je veux dire que...   _____

Answers p. 176

Agreeing and disagreeing

Agreeing	*Disagreeing*
oui	**oui, mais...**
c'est vrai	**ce n'est pas vrai / c'est faux**
tout à fait	**pas du tout**
absolument	**au contraire**
tu as / vous avez raison	**tu as / vous avez tort**
(you are right)	(you are wrong)
je suis d'accord (avec toi)	**je ne suis pas d'accord (avec toi)**

13 See if you can remember the French for the following:

a   That's not true.   _____

b   I don't agree with you (**vous**) _____

c   You (**tu**) are right.   _____

d   You (**vous**) are wrong.   _____

e   I mean that...   _____

f   In my opinion...   _____

g   Not at all.   _____

Answers p. 176

14 What would be your political manifesto? Use some of the phrases from this unit to produce it – or, if you prefer, to produce an outrageous manifesto on someone else's behalf.

Start by stating your top priority:

A mon avis, le/la _____ est primordial(e).

Then go on to write a few more sentences, some of which might begin:

Je crois que...
Je pense qu'il faut...
On devrait...

You may find useful such expressions as:

améliorer	**les conditions économiques**
(to improve)	**les hôpitaux**
	la formation professionnelle
	l'enseignement des langues
prendre des mesures pour	**promouvoir la paix et la justice**
	encourager l'économie
	réduire le chômage
	combattre la faim dans le monde
	sauvegarder l'environnement
lutter contre	**les inégalités sociales**
(to struggle against)	**la drogue**
	le tabac
	l'alcoolisme
maintenir/interdire	**les armes nucléaires**
	les écoles privées
	la liberté d'expression

The recording gives a sample manifesto produced to this pattern.

If you are working with someone else, go on to read your manifesto aloud, giving your partner the opportunity to express agreement or disagreement with each of your points. Again, the relevant phrases for this are on the page opposite (**Tout à fait!** / **Pas du tout!** / etc.).

Answers p. 176

ANSWERS

EXERCISE 1

(a) la réalité du chômage **(b)** les contrats à durée déterminée **(c)** les domaines saisonniers **(d)** le nombre des demandeurs d'emploi **(e)** à plein temps **(f)** le temps partiel **(g)** ajouter **(h)** environ

EXERCISE 2

travailles / cinquante / vivre / demande / difficile / beaucoup / chômage / inquiétant / d'argent / temps / répartir / voulais

EXERCISE 4

(a) Marianne **(b)** Marianne **(c)** Marianne **(d)** Jean-Pierre **(e)** Jean-Pierre **(f)** Marianne

EXERCISE 6

(a) i. 2 euros ii. 1 euro **(b)** The Chamber of Commerce and Industry **(c)** 7 October **(d)** l'hyper-centre

EXERCISE 9

(a) 4 **(b)** 9 **(c)** 1 **(d)** 6 **(e)** 8 **(f)** 3 **(g)** 5 **(h)** 2 **(i)** 7

EXERCISE 10

(a) heureusement **(b)** complètement **(c)** profondément **(d)** doucement **(e)** énormément **(f)** fraîchement **(g)** personnellement

EXERCISE 12

(a) in my opinion… **(b)** personally… **(c)** I think that… **(d)** I believe that… **(e)** I know that… **(f)** it is certain that… **(g)** I mean that…

EXERCISE 13

(a) Ce n'est pas vrai / C'est pas vrai **(b)** Je ne suis pas d'accord avec vous. **(c)** Tu as raison. **(d)** Vous avez tort. **(e)** Je veux dire que… **(f)** A mon avis… **(g)** Pas du tout.

EXERCISE 14

Sample manifesto (given on recording):
   A mon avis, la liberté, l'égalité et la fraternité sont primordiales. Je crois que tout le monde a droit à une bonne éducation et je pense qu'il faut améliorer la formation professionnelle; d'ailleurs, ça réduirait le chômage. Nous devons aussi prendre des mesures pour combattre la faim dans le monde: ce sont nos frères et nos sœurs qui meurent de faim. On devrait lutter contre les inégalités sociales de toutes sortes partout dans le monde. Évidemment, ça coûterait cher, tout ça, mais, si on interdisait les armes nucléaires, on trouverait l'argent nécessaire.

12

INVITATIONS and
REVIEW OF THE COURSE

WHAT YOU WILL LEARN

▶ giving and responding to invitations
▶ making appreciative comments about someone's house
▶ practising the language you have met throughout the course

POINTS TO REMEMBER

You deserve congratulations for working all the way through the course: it represents a great deal of work and has required considerable perseverance. Well done!

Do protect your investment of time and energy by keeping up your French after the end of the course: if you don't, you will be horrified at how quickly you forget what you have laboured to learn.

Here are some suggestions on how to do it:

■ Read French magazines and newspapers.
■ Watch French satellite television and French films on British TV.
■ Listen to French-language radio.
■ Telephone your friends in France.
■ Take every opportunity to meet French people in this country, perhaps through town-twinning activities or French circles.
■ Replay the Conversations of this course, perhaps while you are driving or doing housework.
■ Tap into French Internet sources. Many of the best search engines (e.g. AltaVista) give the option of searching for material in French. Toulouse alone has over 55,000 site-references; try starting with Bienvenue à Toulouse: http://www.mairie-toulouse.fr/
The Paris pages can be accessed on: http://www.paris.org/parisF.html
■ And, **bien sûr**, start on Macmillan's course Breakthrough French 3: Further French!

BEFORE YOU BEGIN

The language you have learned in the course should enable you to develop friendships in French – and one of the things that happens then is that people invite you to their homes. What you need then linguistically, more than anything, is the ability to make appreciative noises in French. This unit will help you with that.

The unit then goes on to review what you have learned throughout the course. You would do well to take your time over that part, looking back to the other units and refreshing your memory on the key words and phrases

An invitation to dinner

LISTEN FOR...

une chorale	a choir
convenir	to agree, to suit
des aliments	foodstuffs

Mme Gibert	Monsieur, pourrais-je vous inviter un soir à dîner? Nous pourrions continuer notre conversation.
M. Pallin	Ah, c'est très gentil, Madame, parce que je suis à Toulouse depuis peu de temps et je connais bien mon milieu professionnel, mais je connais encore peu de familles.
Mme Gibert	Voilà donc une, une bonne occasion. Auriez-vous un soir de libre, disons dans le courant de la semaine prochaine?
M. Pallin	Oh oui! Il n'y a que le mardi, où je me suis inscrit à une chorale, et donc je vais essayer de, d'y aller, mais les autres jours, je suis libre.
Mme Gibert	Bon, nous pouvons convenir de mercredi, vers 20h?
M. Pallin	Ah oui, avec plaisir, oui, oui, merci beaucoup.
Mme Gibert	Bon, ben, parfait. Juste une dernière question: est-ce qu'il y a des aliments que vous ne mangez pas?
M. Pallin	Je mange de tout, mais je n'aime pas du tout les bananes, donc je m'en dispense volontiers.
Mme Gibert	Bon, ben, c'est parfait. J'essayerai de…de trouver un menu qui vous convienne et j'espère que nous passerons une bonne soirée.
M. Pallin	Merci beaucoup.
Mme Gibert	Au revoir, Monsieur.
M. Pallin	Au revoir, Madame.

VOCABULARY

l'occasion (f.)	opportunity
avec plaisir	with pleasure

pourrais-je vous inviter un soir à dîner?
could I invite you to dinner one evening?
Dîner here is actually the verb 'to dine', but the noun is spelt the same: **le dîner**. At midday, the meal is **le déjeuner** and the verb 'to have lunch' is also **déjeuner**.

je suis à Toulouse depuis peu de temps
I have been in Toulouse only a short time (literally I am in Toulouse since little of time). A reminder that French uses the present tense with **depuis**:

Je travaille à Paris depuis vingt ans.
I have been working in Paris for twenty years.

je connais encore peu de familles I don't know many families yet.

disons dans le courant de la semaine prochaine let's say in the course of next week.

Il n'y a que le mardi, où je me suis inscrit à une chorale It's only on Tuesdays, when I have joined a choir [that I am busy].
S'inscrire à means 'to enrol in' or 'sign up for' (something). **L'inscription** means 'enrolment'.

nous pouvons convenir de mercredi we can agree on Wednesday. **Convenir de** is 'to agree on'.

Je mange de tout I eat (some of) everything.

je m'en dispense volontiers I willingly do without them (I willingly let myself off them).

un menu qui vous convienne a menu which suits you. **Convienne** is a subjunctive form of the verb **convenir**. Learn the commoner forms:

Ça vous convient? Does that suit you?
Ça me convient. That suits me.

PRACTICE

1 Here is the sort of thank-you letter Monsieur Pallin might have sent his hostess after the dinner-party. The style seems over-the-top to an English-speaker, but it is quite normal in French. The words missing are:

> occasion   filles   sentiments   soirée   gentillesse
> connaissance   dîner

See if you can write the correct one in each of the gaps.

Chère Madame,

Quelle belle _____ j'ai passée hier! Je vous remercie très

chaleureusement de votre gentille invitation. Votre _____ était parfait:

j'adore le poisson et votre saumon était vraiment exquis! Étant depuis peu de temps à

Toulouse, j'ai également beaucoup apprécié l' _____ de rencontrer

quelques Toulousains – et surtout des Toulousains aussi sympathiques. Vos

_____ sont charmantes, toutes les deux, et cela m'a fait un grand

plaisir de faire la _____ de Monsieur et de Madame Carpentier, qui

sont, eux aussi, d'une _____ exceptionnelle.

> *En vous remerciant de nouveau, chère Madame, je vous prie de croire à mes*

_____ dévoués,

> > *Yves Pallin*

Answers p. 192

2 More gaps to fill in – this time working by ear. This recording is an authentic one in which Annie introduces two of her guests to each other.

Annie   Roger, voici mon _____ Sophie Gourbal.

Sophie   Bonsoir, Monsieur.

Roger   Mes hommages, Madame.

Annie   Et, Sophie, _____ Roger Vaillant. C'est un très
_____ ami de la _____

Roger   Vous habitez Toulouse, vous aussi?

Sophie   Oui, j'habite Toulouse _____ très longtemps.
Vous êtes originaire de... (de la région)?

Roger   Ah non, non, non. Nous _____ de Paris, mais

Answers p. 192   nous _____ ici depuis _____ ans.

3 In this recording, a new acquaintance invites you to dinner in his flat. Follow Philippe's prompts.

CONVERSATION 2

 What a lovely room!

Nicole	Oh! quelle belle pièce! Magnifique! Vraiment!
Christine	C'est la première fois que vous venez?
Nicole	Absolument!
Christine	Ah! mais je suis ravie. Entrez, je vous en prie!
Nicole	Merci. Oh, mais…c'est entouré d'objets d'art ici!
Christine	Ah, il y en a quelques uns, oui, effectivement.
Nicole	Et ces peintures?
Christine	Ah! Ces peintures sont un peu différentes. Regardez celle-ci: c'est une, une belle peinture, qui a été faite par un ami d'un grand-oncle de mon mari. C'est sa femme – elle est suisse. Elle a l'air un peu sévère et si vous vous déplacez dans la pièce, elle vous suit du regard – vous avez remarqué?
Nicole	Ah, oui, effectivement. Tout à fait.
Christine	Et c'est vrai que ce masque africain qui est à côté – vous voyez cette poule?
Nicole	Oui, oui.
Christine	En fait, c'est un masque africain et je trouve que ça va très bien avec: c'est un style tout à fait différent, mais ça crée une atmosphère qui est un petit peu exotique et c'est assez intéressant dans cette pièce…
Nicole	C'est le moins qu'on puisse dire! C'est un contraste, mais, bon, un contraste qui est bien associé. Je vois d'autres pièces, justement, d'Afrique…
Christine	Vous voulez parler d'Oscar? Je l'ai appelé Oscar.
Nicole	En plus!
Christine	Oui! Oscar est une statue…africaine, effectivement, qui, elle aussi, détonne dans cette maison du dix-neuvième siècle, mais permet de mélanger les styles pour ne pas rester trop conventionnel.

> ## LISTEN FOR…
>
> | | |
> |---|---|
> | **ces peintures** | these/those paintings |
> | **ce masque africain** | this/that African mask |
> | **cette poule** | this/that hen |

Vocabulary

la pièce	room, piece, item
ravi(e)	delighted
entouré(e)	surrounded
suisse	Swiss
remarquer	to notice
à côté	alongside
détonner	to be out of place
mélanger	to mix

C'est la première fois que vous venez? Is it the first time you have come? French uses the present tense for this, because the visit is happening now.

je vous en prie please. **Je vous en prie** is also a polite response when you are thanked for something, when it corresponds to 'Don't mention it.'

il y en a quelques uns there are a few of them.

celle-ci this one here. The masculine is **celui-ci**. Learn also **celle-là** and **celui-là**, meaning 'that one there'.

qui a été faite par un ami d'un grand-oncle de mon mari which was done by a friend of a great-uncle of my husband (!).

Elle a l'air un peu sévère She looks a bit severe. **Avoir l'air** + an adjective is the usual way to describe how someone or something looks: **tu as l'air fatigué** 'you look tired'.

si vous vous déplacez dans la pièce, elle vous suit du regard if you move around the room, her eyes follow you (literally if you move yourself in the room, her she you follows with the look). **Se déplacer** is 'to move'.

ça va très bien avec it goes very well with (it). It is very colloquial to end the phrase with **avec**, rather than **avec la peinture**.

ça crée une atmosphère it creates an atmosphere. **Créer** is the verb 'to create'.

C'est le moins qu'on puisse dire! Very much so!/That's putting it mildly! (literally That is the least that one could say!) **Puisse** is a subjunctive form of **pouvoir**.

un contraste qui est bien associé a happy contrast.

En plus! Even better! (literally In addition!)

pour ne pas rester trop conventionnel so as not to remain too conventional.

4 You probably remember that

- **ce** is used before most masculine singular nouns
- **cet** is used before a masculine singular noun beginning with a vowel sound
- **cette** is used before a feminine singular noun
- **ces** is used before a plural noun (masculine or feminine)

Write in the appropriate one before each of the following nouns:

_____ ami

_____ grand-oncle

_____ femme

_____ regard

_____ masque

_____ poule

_____ peintures

_____ pièce

_____ objet d'art

Answers p. 192 _____ maison

5 On the recording is a snatch of conversation between hostess and guest. Play it as many times as you like and, using your pause button, see if you can write out what they say.

Hostess _____

Guest _____

Hostess _____

Guest _____

Hostess _____

Guest _____

Hostess _____

Answers p. 192 Guest _____

6 Getting the intonation right is particularly important when you are trying to sound enthusiastic. The recording for this exercise gives you some good models to imitate. There is one new word: **ravissant** 'delightful'. As you might guess, it is related to **ravi(e)** 'delighted', which you heard in the Conversation.

KEY WORDS
AND PHRASES

pourrais-je vous inviter à dîner?	could I invite you to dinner?
c'est très gentil	that's very kind
je suis à Toulouse depuis peu de temps	I have been in Toulouse only a short time
voilà une bonne occasion	there's a good opportunity
auriez-vous un soir de libre dans le courant de la semaine prochaine?	would you have an evening free in the course of next week?
je me suis inscrit à une chorale	I have enrolled in a choir
les autres jours, je suis libre	the other days, I am free
nous pouvons convenir de mercredi	we can agree on Wednesday
avec plaisir	with pleasure
est-ce qu'il y a des aliments que vous ne mangez pas?	are there any kinds of food that you don't eat?
je mange de tout	I eat everything
oh! quelle belle pièce!	oh! what a beautiful room!
magnifique!	magnificent!
c'est la première fois que vous venez?	is it the first time that you (have) come?
je suis ravie	I am delighted
c'est ravissant	it is delightful
entrez, je voue en prie!	please come in!
ces peintures sont un peu différentes	these paintings are a bit different
vous avez remarqué?	have you noticed?
effectivement	indeed
tout à fait	absolutely
ça va très bien avec	it goes very well
ça crée une atmosphère	it creates an atmosphere
pour ne pas rester trop conventionnel	so as not to remain too conventional

The remainder of the unit gives you an opportunity to go over some of the language covered in the course. You would do well to look through the Key words and phrases of all the units before you tackle the exercises.

7 Madame Lemoine works for a radio station. She had hired a car to go into the forest (**la forêt**) to record the birds (**les oiseaux**) but, while she was there, the car was stolen. On the recording, she reports the loss to the car-hire agent. See how many of the questions you can answer before you look at the transcript below. Most of the language can be found in the Key words and phrases of Units 1–5. New expression: **avoir peur** 'to be afraid' (literally to have fear).

a Name three of the things which are wrong with the car now:

_____

_____

_____

b Where was the car found? _____

c How far away from the car-hire agency was the part of the forest where the car was stolen?

_____

d Was Madame Lemoine alone in the forest by choice? _____

e At what time had she set out to go to the forest? _____

f How long did she stay there? _____

g How long did she have to walk before she got a lift? _____

h Why can't she produce her papers? _____

i What does the car-hire agent suggest they do before going to the police station?

_____

Agent
Ah! Madame Lemoine! Je suis content de vous voir!

Mme Lemoine
Monsieur! On m'a volé la voiture!

Agent
Je sais! Les gendarmes m'ont téléphoné: ils l'ont retrouvée.

Mme Lemoine
Ah bon? Elle est en bon état? Elle démarre encore?

Agent
Non, elle n'est pas en bon état – les portes et les phares sont cassés, il n'y a plus de pneus et il manque des pièces. On a retrouvé la voiture dans la mer!

Mme Lemoine
Dans la mer!

Agent
Oui, alors je suis ravi de vous revoir – j'avais vraiment peur pour vous. Alors, dites-moi ce qui s'est passé: où est-ce que cela a eu lieu?

Mme Lemoine
Dans la forêt, à vingt kilomètres d'ici.

Agent
Dans la forêt? C'est dangereux! Qu'est-ce que vous faisiez là-bas?

Mme Lemoine
Je travaille pour la radio et je voulais faire des enregistrements dans la forêt: les oiseaux surtout. Je sais que c'est dangereux, alors j'ai essayé de trouver quelqu'un pour venir avec moi, mais je n'ai pas pu. Donc j'y suis allée toute seule.

Agent

Vous êtes partie quand?

Mme Lemoine

Vers huit heures ce matin et je me suis arrêtée dans la forêt vers huit heures et demie. Je suis restée trois heures là-bas et puis j'ai voulu rentrer, seulement la voiture n'était plus là. Et il n'y avait personne sur la route, alors il m'a fallu revenir à pied. En fin de compte, une voiture est arrivée une demi-heure plus tard, alors on m'a ramenée jusqu'ici. Alors, voici les clés de la voiture!

Agent

Malheureusement, c'est un petit peu plus compliqué que ça. J'ai besoin de vos papiers.

Mme Lemoine

Mais…mes papiers étaient dans la voiture!

Agent

Ah! Alors il nous faudra aller ensemble à la gendarmerie. Mais d'abord, permettez-moi de vous inviter à prendre un verre au café d'à côté. Je suis sûr que vous en avez besoin pour vous remettre de toutes ces émotions.

Mme Lemoine

Avec plaisir! C'est très gentil, Monsieur.

Answers p. 192

8 This letter is from the author to her brother and future sister-in-law, who have chosen the island of Reunion for their honeymoon (**le voyage de noces**). The language includes many of the Key words and phrases from Units 1–5.

> *Ma chère Véronique,*
> *Mon cher Christophe,*
>
> *Un grand merci pour votre lettre. Je suis ravie d'apprendre que vous avez choisi la Réunion pour votre voyage de noces. Vous me demandez ce que j'ai vu de beau pendant les deux ans que j'ai vécus là-bas et ce que vous devez visiter. Alors…*
>
> *Je n'ai pas visité tout le pays, même en deux ans, mais j'ai vu beaucoup de choses. Tout d'abord, il faut louer une voiture. Faites le tour de l'île – c'est très intéressant. Il y a des plages à Saint-Gilles, à Saint-Leu (qui est un petit peu moins touristique) et puis dans le sud de l'île: allez vous baigner (c'est bien surtout avec un masque et un tuba), mais ne restez pas tout le temps sur la plage, parce que ce qu'il y a de mieux à la Réunion, c'est la montagne, qui est magnifique. La Réunion est un pays à la végétation très variée: en montagne c'est sauvage, au bord de la mer il y a des palmiers et des fleurs tropicales et puis autour du volcan c'est un paysage lunaire. On visite le volcan à pied, alors mettez des chaussures de marche dans vos bagages. Il faut y aller à six heures du matin, parce que les nuages descendent vers midi et on marche dans le brouillard. Faites attention: n'oubliez pas que Maman s'est cassé le pied là-bas!*
>
> *Je vais vous envoyer des brochures sur la Réunion – vous devrez les recevoir après-demain.*
>
> *Qu'est-ce que je peux vous offrir comme cadeau de mariage? Avez-vous besoin de draps? (Et, si oui, de quel type?) Faites-moi savoir!*
>
> *Gros bisous!*
>
> *Stéphanie*

le volcan   volcano

a How long did the author spend in Reunion? _____

b Which beach does she think touristy? _____

c What items will make bathing more enjoyable? _____

d What is the best thing about Reunion? _____

e Where is there a lunar landscape? _____

f Why do you need to set out at 6 a.m.? _____
_____

g What did the author's mother do there? _____

h What is the author suggesting as a wedding present? _____

Answers p. 192

9 On the recording, Mme Lemoine and Agent arrange to go out to dinner. See if you can complete the transcript of their conversation: all the missing elements are Key words and phrases from Units 6–10.

Marianne	Qu'est-ce que tu fais ce week-end?
Jean-Pierre	_____ , faire le ménage, écrire des lettres.
Marianne	_____ Samedi soir, par exemple.
Jean-Pierre	_____
Marianne	On pourrait dîner ensemble. _____
Jean-Pierre	_____ Où veux-tu aller?
Marianne	_____ au restaurant en face de ton bureau?
Jean-Pierre	Oh non, j'y vais souvent à midi. _____ au nouveau restaurant qu'on a construit _____ ; ça s'appelle la Péniche.
Marianne	Je n'en ai pas entendu parler, mais _____ très bien. _____
Jean-Pierre	Oh, _____ , si tu veux?
Marianne	Ça serait _____ , parce que ma voiture à moi _____ Tu viens vers quelle heure?
Jean-Pierre	Oh, sept heures et demie?
Marianne	Très bien. _____
Jean-Pierre	Pas de problème! Il y a un parking au restaurant.
Marianne	Parfait! Alors, à samedi!
Jean-Pierre	A samedi, Marianne!

Answers p. 192

10

This speaking exercise is very similar to the conversation in Exercise 9. You can translate 'we could' as either **nous pourrions** or **on pourrait**.

11

As before, the crossword takes no account of accents.

Across

1. Recording (14)
6. And (2)
7. Wild (7)
10. The (3)
12. Month (4)
13. Oneself (2)
14. To create (5)
18. Street (3)
19. To wish for (7)
20. That (2)
22. And (2)
23. Job (6)
24. Plane (5)
25. Is it **le** or la **pneu**? (2)
26. Reason/right (6)
28. Of it (2)
29. To come in (6)
30. To sleep (6)
33. Place (7)
35. Your (3)
37. State (4)
38. To bury (8)
43. To open (6)
44. Hard (f.) (4)
45. To live (5)
46. To see (4)
47. To catch (8)

Down

1. Efficient (8)
2. To remain (6)
3. Trade (6)
4. And (2)
5. Very (4)
8. Year (2)
9. Programme (8)
11. Week (7)
15. Had (2)
16. Prefix meaning 'again' (2)
17. Brake (5)
19. = **du** before vowel (2, 1)
21. To wait for (8)
23. To write (6)
24. Future (6)
25. Is it **le** or **la chômage**? (2)
27. Letter (6)
31. Forbidden (8)
32. Year (2)
33. Summer (3)
34. Said (3)
35. Found (6)
36. To know (6)
39. Born (f.) (3)
40. Wish, desire (5)
41. Bank (of river) (4)
42. Nothing (4)

Answers p. 192

If working through this course has made you want to visit Toulouse, you may find the following information useful:

> ## Office de Tourisme/Syndicat d'Initiative,
> ## Donjon du Capitole, Square Charles de Gaulle, 31000 Toulouse
> ## Tél. 05.61.11.02.22 Fax 05.61.22.03.63
> **Service 'Accueil de France': où vous pourrez réserver une chambre d'hôtel, vous documenter et trouver tous les services d'une agence de voyage.**
>
> ## Comité Départemental du Tourisme,
> ## 14, rue Bayard, 31000 Toulouse
> ## Tél. 05.61.99.44.00 Fax 05.61.99.44.19
> **Tout ce que vous devez savoir pour séjourner en Haute-Garonne; les gîtes ruraux, les campings à la ferme, les villages de vacances, les gîtes de groupes, les hôtels, les activités de loisirs...**

La Haute-Garonne is the name of the **département** of which Toulouse is the administrative centre.

12 In this speaking exercise, you have twelve lines to say: one relating to each unit of the course. As that is quite a challenging task, you will probably want to think out – and perhaps write out – your answers in advance, so here is the text of the conversation on the recording. The relevant unit numbers are given alongside each of your lines so that you can look things up.

Jean-Pierre Est-ce que tu as déjà pris tes vacances cette année?
You I took a week in the month of August.

Unit 1: _____

Jean-Pierre Et qu'est-ce que tu as fait?
You I went to Toulouse.

Unit 2: _____

Jean-Pierre Et c'était comment, Toulouse au mois d'août?
You It was very interesting, but it was very humid.

Unit 3: _____

Jean-Pierre Oui, ça, c'est pas très agréable.
You And you, what did you do during the holidays?

Unit 4: _____

Jean-Pierre Moi, je n'ai pas encore pris de vacances. J'ai envie de partir la semaine prochaine mais je ne sais pas où aller.
You Go to Toulouse! It's very beautiful.

Unit 5: _____

Jean-Pierre	J'ai plutôt envie d'aller au bord de la mer, mais je n'aime pas partir seul en vacances. Ça ne te dit pas de venir avec moi?
You	Why not? Yes, I'll come with you!
	Unit 6: _____

Jean-Pierre	Ah! ben très bien! Et où irons-nous?
You	We could do the world tour!
	Unit 7: _____

Jean-Pierre	Oui…si on gagnait au Loto!
You	Do you fancy going to Australia?
	Unit 8: _____

Jean-Pierre	Oh non! C'est trop loin!
You	And, in addition, I've lost my passport!
	Unit 9: _____

Jean-Pierre	Oh! quelle catastrophe!
You	Yes! …You know, we could hire a boat on the Canal du Midi.
	Unit 10: _____

Jean-Pierre	Ça, c'est une bonne idée – si c'est pas trop tard.
You	What do you mean?
	Unit 11: _____

Jean-Pierre	J'aimerais partir la semaine prochaine – je ne sais pas si c'est trop tard pour faire une réservation.
You	I am free today. I could try to find something.
	Unit 12: _____

Jean-Pierre	Parfait! Je serai ravi si tu réussis!

Answers p. 192

13 The tasks below are numbered to correspond to the twelve units of the course. They would be best carried out with a partner, but, with a little imagination, could be tackled on your own.

1. Give an account of something you have done, perhaps a project for work or a course of study.
2. Recount a past holiday or business trip.
3. Describe how things were in your childhood.
4. Ask survey-type questions about the other person's family, profession, home, etc.
5. Give instructions on how to set the time on your watch/how to use a pocket calculator/how to get to a particular place in the building.
6. Say what you will be doing over the next year.
7. Say what you would do if you were very rich.
8. Make arrangements to go out together.
9. Roleplay a disaster of your choice (lost passport or whatever).
10. Say something about your local town.
11. Discuss either unemployment or improvements to transport.
12. Invite the other person for a meal.

You have now reached the end of the course– **félicitations**!

EXERCISE 1

soirée / dîner / occasion / filles / connaissance / gentillesse / sentiments

EXERCISE 2

amie / voici / vieil (It is vieux before most masculine singular nouns, vieil before a masculine singular noun beginning with a vowel sound, vieille before a feminine singular noun and vieux or vieilles in the plural.)/ famille / depuis / sommes / habitons / vingt-cinq

EXERCISE 4

cet ami / ce grand-oncle / cette femme / ce regard / ce masque / cette poule / ces peintures / cette pièce / cet objet d'art / cette maison

EXERCISE 5

Entrez! Entrez! / (Oh!) Quelle belle pièce! / Merci! / C'est magnifique! / C'est très gentil! / Cette peinture est charmante! / Oui, moi aussi, j'aime beaucoup cette peinture. / C'est très, très beau!

EXERCISE 7

(a) Three out of: doors broken, lights broken, no tyres, parts missing   (b) In the sea   (c) About 20 km
(d) No (She had tried to find someone to go with her.)
(e) 8 a.m.   (f) 3 hours   (g) Half an hour
(h) They were in the car   (i) Go and have a drink at a café

EXERCISE 8

(a) Two years   (b) Saint-Gilles   (c) Mask and snorkel   (d) The mountain(s)   (e) Round the volcano   (f) The clouds come down and you are walking in fog   (g) Break her foot   (h) Sheets

EXERCISE 9

Je pensais rester chez moi / Tu n'as pas envie de sortir? / Ça dépend – pour quoi faire? / Ça te dit? / Pourquoi pas? / Nous pourrions peut-être aller / Moi, j'aimerais mieux aller / au bord du canal / ça me va / On se donne rendez-vous où? / je passe chez toi / gentil / est en panne / Et comment on va faire pour se garer?

EXERCISE 11

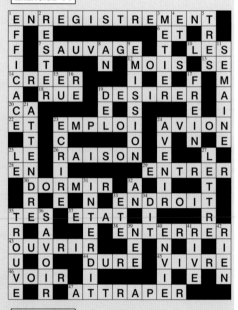

EXERCISE 12

(1) J'ai pris une semaine au mois d'août.
(2) Je suis allée à Toulouse.   (3) C'était très intéressant, mais c'était très humide.   (4) Et toi, qu'est-ce que tu as fait pendant les vacances?
(5) Va à Toulouse! C'est très beau.   (6) Pourquoi pas? Oui, je viendrai avec toi!   (7) Nous pourrions faire le tour du monde!   (8) As-tu envie d'aller en Australie?   (9) Et, en plus, j'ai perdu mon passeport!   (10) Oui!…Tu sais, nous pourrions louer un bateau sur le canal du Midi.   (11) Qu'est-ce que tu veux dire?   (12) Je suis libre aujourd'hui. Je pourrais essayer de trouver quelque chose.

REFERENCE SECTION

This section contains

- definitions of grammatical terms such as 'nouns' and 'articles'
- a list of the numbers in French
- tables of all the verbs in the course
- a French–English vocabulary
- a list of the grammar covered in each unit of the course, along with the titles of the Conversations
- an index of page-references to grammar points

GLOSSARY OF GRAMMATICAL TERMS

Verbs

A VERB expresses action or being:

| The dog *is eating* the meat. | I *am*. | Mary *hates* football. |
| **Le chien *mange* la viande.** | **Je *suis*.** | **Marie *déteste* le football.** |

- The SUBJECT of a verb is the person or thing performing the action of the verb:

| *The dog* is eating the meat. | *I* am. | *Mary* hates football. |
| **Le *chien* mange la viande.** | **Je suis.** | **Marie déteste le football.** |

- The OBJECT of a verb is the person or thing on the receiving end:

| The dog is eating *the meat*. | I am. | Mary hates *football*. |
| **Le chien mange *la viande*.** | **Je suis.** | **Marie déteste *le football*.** |

- The INFINITIVE is the form of the verb preceded in English by 'to':

| to eat | to be | to hate |
| **manger** | **être** | **détester** |

- The TENSE indicates whether the action is situated in the past, the present, the future or a hypothetical context.
- PAST PARTICIPLES include:

| eaten | been | hated |
| **mangé** | **été** | **détesté** |

Nouns and gender

A NOUN is the name of a person or thing:

| Mary | dog | meat |
| **Marie** | **chien** | **viande** |

In French, all nouns belong to one of two groups called GENDERS (masculine and feminine). These are often indicated thus:

chien (m.), **viande** (f.).

Articles

French ARTICLES are the equivalents of 'the', 'a', 'an' and 'some':

le, la, l', les, un, une, du, de la, de l', des.

Pronouns

A PRONOUN is a word that stands instead of a noun:

Mary hates football.	▷	She hates *it*.
Marie déteste le football.	▷	**Elle *le* déteste.**

Adjectives

An ADJECTIVE describes a noun or pronoun, e.g.

beautiful	big	green
beau, bel, belle, beaux, belles	**grand(e)(s)**	**vert(e)(s)**

- POSSESSIVE ADJECTIVES are words such as:

my	his/her	our
mon, ma, mes	**son, sa, ses**	**notre, nos**

- DEMONSTRATIVE ADJECTIVES are:

this/that	these/those
ce, cet, cette	**ces**

Adverbs

An ADVERB is a word which modifies the action of a verb:

completely	well	quickly
complètement	**bien**	**vite**

Prepositions

A PREPOSITION is a word or phrase which goes before a noun or pronoun to show its relation to another part of the sentence:

under	next to	without
sous	**à côté de**	**sans**

TABLES OF THE VERBS IN THE COURSE

Notes on verb forms

Present: The forms for **il** and **elle** are identical, as are those for **ils** and **elles**.

Perfect: Present tense of **avoir** or **être** + past participle.

Imperfect: Usually beginning of **nous** form of present tense + endings -**ais**, -**ais**, -**ait**, -**ions**, -**iez**, -**aient**.

Future: Beginning derived from infinitive (or irregular) + endings of present tense of **avoir** (-**ai**, -**as**, -**a**, -**ons**, -**ez**, -**ont**).

Conditional: Beginning of future + endings of imperfect.

Imperative: Often the same as the present tense, but with no -**s** on the **tu** form of -**er** verbs.

		Present	Perfect	Imperfect	Future	Conditional

AVOIR (to have)

		Present	Perfect	Imperfect	Future	Conditional
j'ai	nous avons	j'ai eu	j'avais	j'aurai	j'aurais
tu as	vous avez	etc.	etc.	etc.	etc.
il/elle a	ils/elles ont		Imperative: **aie! ayons! ayez!**		

ÊTRE (to be)

je suis	nous sommes	j'ai été	j'étais	je serai	je serais
tu es	vous êtes	etc.	etc.	etc.	etc.
il est	ils sont		Imperative: **sois! soyons! soyez!**		

HABITER (to work): Model for regular verbs with infinitives ending in **-er**.
Over 200 of these occur in the course. Note that the perfect is formed with **être** in the following verbs: **arriver** (to arrive): **je suis arrivé(e)**, **entrer** (to enter): **je suis entré(e)**, **monter** (to go up): **je suis monté(e)**, **rester** (to stay): **je suis resté(e)**, **tomber** (to fall): **je suis tombé(e)**, **retourner** (to return): **je suis retourné(e)**.

j'habite	nous habitons	j'ai habité	j'habitais	j'habiterai	j'habiterais
tu habites	vous habitez	etc.	etc.	etc.	etc.
il habite	ils habitent		Imperative: **habite! habitons! habitez!**		

FINIR (to finish): Model for regular verbs with infinitives ending in **-ir**, e.g.
bâtir (to build), **enrichir** (to enrich), **fleurir** (to flower), **fournir** (to furnish), **réfléchir** (to reflect, think), **répartir** (to share out), **réunir** (to bring together), **réussir** (to succeed).

je finis	nous finissons	j'ai fini	je finissais	je finirai	je finirais
tu finis	vous finissez	etc.	etc.	etc.	etc.
il finit	ils finissent		Imperative:	**finis! finissons! finissez!**	

VENDRE (to sell): Model for regular verbs with infinitives ending in **-re**, e.g.
attendre (to wait for), **combattre** (to combat), **correspondre** (to correspond), **dépendre** (to depend), **entendre** (to hear), **perdre** (to lose), **rendre** (to give back), **répondre** (to answer), **suspendre** (to suspend); also **mettre** (to put), **permettre** (to permit), **remettre** (to put back, put off), but with past participles **mis**, **permis** and **remis**; also **descendre** (to go down), but with perfect **je suis descendu(e)**.

je vends	nous vendons	j'ai vendu	je vendais	je vendrai	je vendrais
tu vends	vous vendez	etc.	etc.	etc.	etc.
il vend	ils vendent		Imperative: **vends! vendons! vendez!**		

Irregular verbs in -er

		Present	Perfect	Imperfect	Future	Conditional

ALLER (to go)

je vais	nous allons	je suis allé(e)	j'allais	j'irai	j'irais
tu vas	vous allez	etc.	etc.	etc.	etc.
il va	ils vont		Imperative: **va! allons! allez!**		

APPELER (to call): Model for others, including **jeter** (to throw), where the consonant before the **-er** of the infinitive doubles before a 'mute' **-e**.

j'appelle	nous appelons	j'ai appelé	j'appelais	j'appellerai	j'appellerais
tu appelles	vous appelez	etc.	etc.	etc.	etc.
il appelle	ils appellent		Imperative: **appelle! appelons! appelez!**		

	Present	Perfect	Imperfect	Future	Conditional

FAIRE (to do, make): Model for **défaire** (to unmake), **refaire** (to remake)

je fais	nous faisons	j'ai fait	je faisais	je ferai	je ferais
tu fais	vous faites	etc.	etc.	etc.	etc.
il fait	ils font		Imperative: **fais! faisons! faites!**		

LIRE (to read): Model for **relire** (to reread)

je lis	nous lisons	j'ai lu	je lisais	je lirai	je lirais
tu lis	vous lisez	etc.	etc.	etc.	etc.
il lit	ils lisent		Imperative: **lis! lisons! lisez!**		

PRENDRE (to take): Model for **apprendre** (to learn), **comprendre** (to understand)

je prends	nous prenons	j'ai pris	je prenais	je prendrai	je prendrais
tu prends	vous prenez	etc.	etc.	etc.	etc.
il prend	ils prennent		Imperative: **prends! prenons! prenez!**		

SUIVRE (to follow)

je suis	nous suivons	j'ai suivi	je suivais	je suivrai	je suivrais
tu suis	vous suivez	etc.	etc.	etc.	etc.
il suit	ils suivent		Imperative: **suis! suivons! suivez!**		

VIVRE (to live): Model for **survivre** (to survive), **revivre** (to live again)

je vis	nous vivons	j'ai vécu	je vivais	je vivrai	je vivrais
tu vis	vous vivez	etc.	etc.	etc.	etc.
il vit	ils vivent		Imperative: **vis! vivons! vivez!**		

Reflexive verbs

SE LEVER (to get up): All reflexive verbs form their perfect with the verb **être**.
Note that the pronoun in the infinitive is not always **se**:
Je dois me lever/Tu dois te lever/Nous devons nous lever/Vous devez vous lever. In **lever** and **se lever**, as in the verb **espérer**, a grave accent appears before 'mute' **-e**.

Present

je me lève	nous nous levons
tu te lèves	vous vous levez
il se lève	ils se lèvent
elle se lève	elles se lèvent

Perfect

je me suis levé(e)	nous nous sommes levé(e)s
tu t'es levé(e)	vous vous êtes levé(e)(s)
il s'est levé	ils se sont levés
elle s'est levé	elles se sont levées

Imperfect

je me levais	nous nous levions
tu te levais	vous vous leviez
il se levait	ils se levaient
elle se levait	elles se levaient

Future

je me lèverai	nous nous lèverons
tu te lèveras	vous vous lèverez
il se lèvera	ils se lèveront
elle se lèvera	elles se lèveront

Conditional

je me lèverais	nous nous lèverions
tu te lèverais	vous vous lèveriez
il se lèverait	ils se lèveraient
elle se lèverait	elles se lèveraient

Imperative:

lève-toi!
levons-nous!
levez-vous!

NUMBERS

1 un	61 soixante et un
2 deux	62 soixante-deux
3 trois	70 soixante-dix
4 quatre	71 soixante et onze
5 cinq	72 soixante-douze
6 six	73 soixante-treize
7 sept	74 soixante-quatorze
8 huit	75 soixante-quinze
9 neuf	76 soixante-seize
10 dix	77 soixante-dix-sept
11 onze	78 soixante-dix-huit
12 douze	79 soixante-dix-neuf
13 treize	80 quatre-vingts
14 quatorze	81 quatre-vingt-un
15 quinze	82 quatre-vingt-deux
16 seize	83 quatre-vingt-trois
17 dix-sept	90 quatre-vingt-dix
18 dix-huit	91 quatre-vingt-onze
19 dix-neuf	92 quatre-vingt-douze
20 vingt	93 quatre-vingt-treize
21 vingt et un	94 quatre-vingt-quatorze
22 vingt-deux	95 quatre-vingt-quinze
23 vingt-trois	96 quatre-vingt-seize
24 vingt-quatre	97 quatre-vingt-dix-sept
25 vingt-cinq	98 quatre-vingt-dix-huit
26 vingt-six	99 quatre-vingt-dix-neuf
27 vingt-sept	100 cent
28 vingt-huit	101 cent un
29 vingt-neuf	102 cent deux
30 trente	103 cent trois
31 trente et un	150 cent cinquante
32 trente-deux	200 deux cents
40 quarante	201 deux cent un
41 quarante et un	202 deux cent deux
42 quarante-deux	299 deux cent quatre-vingt-dix-neuf
50 cinquante	300 trois cents
51 cinquante et un	333 trois cent trente-trois
52 cinquante-deux	1000 mille
60 soixante	1.000.000 un million

1st, 2nd, 3rd etc. are expressed:

premier/première	neuvième
deuxième (or second(e))	dixième
troisième	onzième
quatrième	douzième
cinquième	...
sixième	vingtième
septième	centième
huitième	millième

VOCABULARY

Many words have more than one meaning, depending on the context in which they are used. You will have to look them up in a dictionary to find the full range of possibilities as this list of vocabulary concentrates mainly on the sense of the words as they are used in the course.

Abbreviations:

adj. = adjective	*adv.* = adverb	*esp.* = especially
f. = feminine	*m.* = masculine	*n.* = noun
p.p. = past participle	*pl.* = plural	*sing.* = singular
usu. = usually		

Adjectives:

■ **blanc(he)** = masculine **blanc**, feminine **blanche**.

■ **amoureux(-euse)** = masculine **amoureux**, feminine **amoureuse**.

■ where only one form is given (e.g. **jeune**), it is used for both the masculine and the feminine.

A

à to, at
  à peu près approximately
  à tout à l'heure! see you later!
abandonner to abandon
abondamment abundantly
d'abord first of all
abri *m.* shelter
absolu(e) absolute
absolument absolutely
accélérer to accelerate
accepter to accept
accès *m.* access
accident *m.* accident
accompagner to accompany
accord *m.* agreement
  d'accord OK, fine, agreed
accueil *m.* welcome
accueillir to welcome
acheter to buy
acte *m.* act
acteur *m.* actor
activité *f.* activity
actrice *f.* actress
actuel(le) current, present
actuellement at the moment
admirer to admire
adresse *f.* address

aéronautique *adj.* aeronautical; *n.f.* aeronautics
aéroport *m.* airport
africain(e) African
âge *m.* age
âgé(e) elderly
agence *f.* agency
agréable pleasant
agriculture *f.* agriculture
agronomie *f.* agronomy
aide *f.* help
aider to help
aile *f.* wing
ailleurs elsewhere
  d'ailleurs moreover
aimable kind
aimer to like, to love
ainsi thus
  ainsi que as well as
air *m.* air, appearance
air conditionné *m.* air conditioning
ajouter to add
alcool *m.* alcohol, spirit
alcoolisme *m.* alcoholism
Algérie *f.* Algeria
alignement *m.* alignment
aliment *m.* foodstuff
aller to go
aller *m.* single/outward journey
allo/allô hello (telephone only)

allonger   to extend, stretch out, lay down
   s'allonger   to grow longer, stretch out, lie down
allumer   to light, turn on
alors   well then, at that time
améliorer   to improve
amener   to lead, to take (someone somewhere)
ami(e)   friend
amitié *f.*   friendship
amoureux(-euse)   in love
ampoule *f.*   bulb
an *m.*   year
ancien(ne)   ancient, former
Angleterre *f.*   England
animal, *pl.* **-aux**, *m.*   animal
année *f.*   year
annonce *f.*   announcement, advertisement
annulation *f.*   cancellation
antenne *f.*   antenna, aerial
août *m.*   August
appareil *m.*   apparatus, esp. telephone or plane
apparemment   apparently
appartement *m.*   flat, apartment
appel *m.*   call
appelé *m.*   conscript
appeler   to call
   s'appeler   to be called
apporter   to bring
apprendre   to learn
approcher   to draw nearer
   s'approcher de   to approach
appuyer   to press
après   after
après-midi *m.* or *f.*   afternoon
arbre *m.*   tree
archaïque   archaic
architectural(e)   architectural
argent *m.*   money
arme *f.*   weapon, arm
aromatique   aromatic
arrêt *m.*   stop
arrêter   to stop
   s'arrêter   to stop (oneself)
arriver   to arrive
art *m.*   art
artisanal(e)   hand-crafted, home-made
ascendants *m.pl.*   ascendants, ancestors
aspect *m.*   aspect
s'asseoir   to sit down
assez   enough, fairly, quite
association *f.*   association
associé(e)   associated
assouplissant *m.*   softener
assurance *f.*   insurance
assuré *m.*   insured person
astucieux(-euse)   clever
atmosphère *f.*   atmosphere
atteindre   to attain
attendre   to wait for
attention *f.*   attention, care
attraper   to catch
au-delà   beyond
au-dessous (de)   underneath
au-dessus (de)   above

aucun(e) (often with **ne**)   no, none
aujourd'hui   today
auprès de   close to, by
aussi   also, as
auteur *m.*   author
autobus *m.*   bus
automatiquement   automatically
automatisme *m.*   automatism, automatic functioning
autour (de)   around
autre   other
auquel (à laquelle), auxquel(le)s   to which, to whom
avancer   to advance
avant   before
avantage *m.*   advantage
avec   with
avenir *m.*   future
aventure *f.*   adventure
avion *m.*   plane
avis *m.*   opinion
avoir   to have

B

bagages *m.pl.*   luggage
baigner   to bathe (someone or something)
   se baigner   to bathe (oneself)
baisser   to lower, become lower
   se baisser   to stoop
ballon *m.*   ball, balloon
bancaire *adj.*   bank
banque *f.*   bank
bar *m.*   bar
basilique *f.*   basilica
bastide *f.*   in SW France: walled town; in Provence: solidly built house
bateau *m.*   boat
bâtir   to build
batterie *f.*   battery
bavette *f.*   sirloin
beau (belle)   beautiful, handsome
beaucoup   a lot, very much
beau-frère *m.*   brother-in-law, step-brother
bébé *m.*   baby
bégonia *m.*   begonia
belle-sœur *f.*   sister-in-law, step-sister
béquille *f.*   crutch
Berbère *m./f.*   Berber
besoin *m.*   need
   avoir besoin de   to need
bête *adj.*   stupid; *n.f.* beast
bien   well
   bien à toi   best wishes (in a letter)
   bien entendu   of course
bientôt   soon
binational(e)   binational
biologie *f.*   biology
bisou *m.*   kiss
   gros bisous   lots of love (in a letter)
blanc(he)   white
blé *m.*   corn

---

blessé *m.* injured person
blesser to injure, wound, hurt
blessure *f.* wound
bleu(e) blue
blond(e) blond
   bière blonde lager
bloquer to block
boire to drink
bois *m.* wood
boisson *f.* drink
boîte *f.* box, can
   boîte de vitesses gear-box
bord *m.* edge
   au bord de la mer at the seaside
boucher to block
bouchon *m.* top, stopper, cork
   bouchon de réservoir d'essence petrol cap
bouger to move
bougie *f.* candle, spark plug
bouilloire *f.* kettle
bouleverser to bowl over, overwhelm, shatter
bouton *m.* button
brancher to plug in
bras *m.* arm
bricoler to fix, tinker with, do DIY
brillamment brilliantly
brillant(e) brilliant
bris *m.* breaking
britannique British
brocart *m.* brocade
brochure *f.* brochure
brouillard *m.* fog
bru *f.* daughter-in-law
budget *m.* budget
bungalow *m.* bungalow, chalet

C

c'est-à-dire that is to say
ça (abbreviation of **cela**) that
   ça te dit? / ça vous dit? do you fancy that?
   ça va? / ça va are you all right? / I'm all right
   ça y est! got it! done it!
cabine téléphonique *f.* telephone kiosk
câbles *m.* **de démarrage** jump-leads
cadre *m.* frame, context, executive
café *m.* café, coffee
café-théâtre *m.* theatre workshop
caler to stall
calme calm, quiet
campagne *f.* country
camping *m.* camping, campsite
cantine *f.* canteen
capitale *f.* capital city
capitoul *m.* magistrate (in Toulouse)
carburant *m.* fuel
carrière *f.* career, quarry
carte *f.* card, map
   carte bancaire bank card
   carte de crédit credit card
   carte d'identité identity card
   carte grise vehicle registration document

cartographie *f.* cartography
cas *m.* case
   en cas de in case of
   en tout cas anyway, in any case
case *f.* square, hut
casser to break
cassette *f.* cassette
cathédrale *f.* cathedral
cave *f.* cellar
ce que that which
cela that (see also **ça**)
célèbre famous
celui-ci (celle-ci) this one
celui-là (celle-là) that one
centaine *f.* about a hundred
centenaire hundred-year-old
centime *m.* centime (one-hundredth of a franc)
centre *m.* centre
centre-ville *m.* town centre
cependant however
certes certainly
certificat *m.* certificate
ce, cet (before vowel) **(cette)** this, that
ces these, those
chacun(e) each
chaleureux (-euse) warm
chaleureusement warmly
chambre *f.* room, bedroom, chamber
   chambre d'hôte room in a guesthouse
champ *m.* field
chance *f.* luck, opportunity
changement *m.* change
changer to change
chaque each
charbon *m.* coal
charge *f.* charge, load, responsibility
charmant(e) charming
chasse *f.* hunt, hunting
chasser to hunt
chaud(e) hot
chauffage central *m.* central heating
chauffe-eau *m.* water-heater
chaussure *f.* shoe
chemin *m.* way, path
   chemin de halage towpath
cheminée *f.* chimney, fireplace
chêne *m.* oak
chèque *m.* cheque
   chèque de voyage travellers' cheque
cher (chère) dear, expensive
chercher to look for
chercheur *m.* researcher
cheval *m.* horse
cheville *f.* ankle
chez (moi) at (my) place
chiffre *m.* figure
Chine *f.* China
choisir to choose
chômage *m.* unemployment
chômeur *m.* unemployed person
ci-dessus above (in text)
ciment *m.* cement
cimetière *m.* cemetery

---

circuit *m.* circuit, tour
circulation *f.* traffic
cité *f.* city
citer to cite
clair(e) clear, light
clandestin *m.* illegal immigrant
classement *m.* classification, filing
clé/clef *f.* key
client(e) client
climat *m.* climate
cloître *m.* cloister
club *m.* club
code *m.* code
    se mettre en code to dip headlights
cœur *m.* heart
collecter to collect
collectif(-ive) collective
collègue *m.* or *f.* colleague
combattre to combat
combien how much, how many
comité *m.* committee
comme as, like
commencer to start
comment how, what
commerçant *m.* trader
commerce *m.* commerce, trade
commission *f.* commission
commun(e) common
    transports en commun public transport
communauté *f.* community
compagnie *f.* company
complet(-ète) complete
complètement completely
compliqué(e) complicated
comprendre to understand, include
compter to count
comte *m.* count
conception f. conception
concert *m.* concert
concertation *f.* dialogue, consultation, concerted action
concitoyen *m.* fellow citizen
concours *m.* competitive examination
concubin(e) partner, co-habitee
condition *f.* condition
conduire to drive
confier to entrust
confort *m.* comfort
congrès *m.* congress
conjoint(e) spouse
connaissance *f.* knowledge, acquaintance
consacrer consecrate, devote
conseiller to advise
conseiller(-ère) adviser, consultant, councillor, counsellor
conserver to conserve, preserve, keep
consister à to consist in
consommer to consume
constamment constantly
constant(e) constant
construction *f.* construction
construire to build
contact *m.* contact

contempler to contemplate
contemporain(e) contemporary
content(e) content, happy
contestable arguable
contexte *m.* context
contraire *m.* contrary, opposite
    au contraire on the contrary
contrairement à unlike
contrat *m.* contract
contre against
    par contre on the other hand
contrôle *m.* control, check
convaincre to convince
convenir de to agree on
conventionnel(le) conventional
copain (copine) friend
corallien(ne) *adj.* coral
corps *m.* body
correspondant(e) correspondent, opposite number
correspondre à to correspond to
côte *f.* rib, coast
côté *m.* side
    à côté de alongside
cou *m.* neck
couche *f.* layer, coat (of paint), nappy
coucher to lay down
    se coucher to lie down, go to bed
coude *m.* elbow
couler to flow
coup *m.* blow, stroke
    d'un seul coup at a stroke
    tout d'un coup suddenly
couper to cut
courage *m.* courage
courant *m.* current, course
    dans le courant de in the course of
courir to run
courroie *f.* **de ventilateur** fan belt
cours *m.* course, class
    cours du soir evening class
course *f.* race, errand and *esp. pl.* shopping
coûter to cost
couvent *m.* convent, religious house
couverture *f.* cover, blanket
couvrir to cover
création *f.* creation
créer to create
croire to believe
croisé *adj.* crossed; *n.m.* crusader
croisière *f.* cruise
cuisine *f.* kitchen
culture *f.* culture
culturel(le) cultural
cycle *m.* cycle
cyclisme *m.* cycling

D

---

d'abord first of all
danger *m.* danger
dangereux(-euse) dangerous
dans in

---

dansant(e) *adj.* dancing
danser to dance
date *f.* date
débrouiller to cope, get by
début *m.* start
décembre *m.* December
décès *m.* decease
décider to decide
décision *f.* decision
décor *m.* decor
découverte *f.* discovery
découvrir to discover
dedans inside
défavorisé(e) underprivileged
définition *f.* definition
dehors outside
déjà already
déjeuner to have lunch; *n.m.* lunch
   petit déjeuner breakfast
demain tomorrow
demander to ask
démarrer to start up, to get going
demi-heure *f.* half an hour
demi-pension *f.* half-board
dépasser to exceed
dépêcher to hurry
dépendre de to depend on, report to
déplacer to move
   se déplacer to move (oneself)
déposer to deposit, hand in
depuis since
   depuis deux ans for the last two years
dernier(-ère) last
dès from the moment of
descendant *m.* descendant
descendre to go down
déséquilibré(e) unbalanced
désolé(e) very sorry
désormais from now on
dessous underneath
dessus above
déterminé fixed, fixed-term
détonner to be out of place
devant before, in front of
développement *m.* development
développer to develop
dévisser to unscrew
devoir to have an obligation, must, should, ought
dévotion *f.* devotion
dévouer to devote
difficile difficult
difficulté *f.* difficulty
digne dignified, worthy
dimension *f.* dimension
dîner to have dinner (evening); *n.m.* dinner
diplôme *m.* diploma
dire to say
directement directly
direction *f.* direction
discuter to discuss
dispenser de to excuse from;
   se dispenser de to avoid, get out of
disponible available, free

dispositions *f. pl.* arrangements
disque *m.* record
distance *f.* distance
distribuer to distribute
diverses various
diviser to divide
divorce *m.* divorce
dizaine *f.* about ten
doigt *m.* finger
domaine *m.* domain
dominer to dominate, overlook
don *m.* gift
donc then
donjon *m.* keep (of a castle)
données *f.pl.* data
donner to give
dont of which, of whom
dormir to sleep
dortoir *m.* dormitory
dossier *m.* file, project
doucement gently, slowly
douche *f.* shower
doux (douce) gentle, soft
dramatique dramatic
drap *m.* sheet
drogue *f.* drug(s)
droit *m.* right;
   avoir le droit de to be allowed to
   tout droit straight on
droit(e) right
   à droite to the right
   sur la droite on the right
dû *p.p.* of **devoir**
dur(e) hard
durant during
durée *f.* duration
durer to last

E

eau *f.* water
école *f.* school
économie *f.* economy, economics
économique economic(al)
écouter to listen to
écrire to write
édifice *m.* edifice, building
éducation *f.* education
effectivement indeed
effectuer to effect, bring about
efficace efficient, effective
efficacité *f.* efficiency, effectiveness
effort *m.* effort
également equally, also
égalité *f.* equality
église *f.* church
égrener to run through, pick off
électricité *f.* electricity
électrochimie *f.* electrochemistry
électronique electronic; *n.f.* electronics
élément *m.* element
élevé(e) high, raised, brought up

embarquer to embark
embouteillage *m.* traffic jam
embrasser to kiss
émetteur *m.* transmitter
émission *f.* broadcast
émotion *f.* emotion
empêcher to prevent
emploi *m.* job, employment
   emploi du temps timetable
en in
   en fait in fact
   en fin de compte in the end
encore still, yet
encourager to encourage
endroit *m.* place
énergie *f.* energy
enfant *usu. m.* child
enfermer to enclose, shut in
enfin at last
engin *m.* machine
énorme enormous
énormément enormously
enregistrement *m.* recording
enrichir to enrich
enseignement *m.* teaching
ensemble together
ensuite next, then
entendre to hear
   entendre parler de to hear tell of
enterrer to bury
entier(-ère) entire
entorse *f.* sprain
entourer to surround
entraîner to drag, pull, lead
entre between
entreprise *f.* firm
entrer to enter
envie *f.* desire, wish
   avoir envie de to want to
environ around, approximately
environnement *m.* environment
envisager to envisage
envoyer to send
épaule *f.* shoulder
époque *f.* period, time
épouser to marry
équitable fair
espace *m.* space
espèce *f.* species, kind
   espèces cash
espérer to hope
essayer to try
essence *f.* (two-star) petrol
essentiel(le) essential
essentiellement essentially
essuie-glace *m.* windscreen wiper
est *m.* east
état *m.* state
   en bon état in good condition
   États-Unis United States
été *m.* summer (also *p.p.* of **être**)
étonner to astonish
être to be

étude *f.* study
étudier to study
eu *p.p.* of **avoir**
évacuer to evacuate
événement *m.* event
évêque *m.* bishop
évidemment obviously
évident(e) evident, obvious
exact(e) exact
excellent(e) excellent
exceptionnel(le) exceptional
exclusion *f.* exclusion
excursion *f.* excursion
excuser to forgive
   s'excuser to apologise
exemple *m.* example
exiger to demand
exister to exist
exotique exotic
expérience *f.* experience, experiment
expert(e) expert; *n.m.* expert
exploitant *m.* *usu.* farmer
exploiter to exploit
exploration *f.* exploration
exposition *f.* exhibition
expression *f.* expression
exquis(e) exquisite
extraire to extract
extrait *m.* extract
extraordinaire extraordinary
extrême extreme
extrêmement extremely

F

face *f.* face, side, heads (of coin)
   en face (de) opposite
facile easy
façon *f.* way
faim *f.* hunger
faire to do, make
   faire la part des choses to distinguish
fait *m.* deed, fact
   en fait in fact, actually
falloir (il faut) to be necessary
famille *f.* family
fatigué(e) tired
faut see **falloir**
fauteuil *m.* armchair
favorable favourable
femme *f.* woman, wife
   femme de ménage cleaning lady
ferme firm; *n. f.* farm
fermer to close
festival *m.* festival
fête *f.* feast-day, party, bank holiday
feu *m.* fire
   feux (rouges) traffic lights
fier(-ère) proud
figurer to figure
fille *f.* girl, daughter
fin *f.* end

en fin de compte   in the end
financier(-ère)   financial
finir   to finish
fleur *f.*   flower
fleurir   to flower
fleuve *m.*   river
foire *f.*   fair
fois *f.*   time
folle (*f.* of **fou**)   mad
fonction *f.*   function, office
   en fonction de   according to
forêt *f.*   forest
formation *f.*   training
forme *f.*   form
formidable   fantastic
fou (folle)   mad
foule *f.*   crowd
fournir   to furnish
foyer *m.*   home, hearth, hostel
fraîchement   freshly
frais (fraîche)   fresh, cool
franchement   frankly, honestly
fraternité *f.*   fraternity
frein *m.*   brake
   frein à main   handbrake
fréquemment   frequently
frère *m.*   brother
froid(e)   cold
   avoir froid   to be cold
frontière *f.*   border
frustré(e)   frustrated
fusible *m.*   fuse
futur *m.*   future

G

gagner   to win, earn
   gagner sa vie   to earn one's living
gai(e)   gay
garagiste *usu. m.*   garage owner
garçon *m.*   boy, young man, bachelor, waiter
garder   to keep
garer (la voiture)   to park (the car)
gâteau *m.*   cake, biscuit
gauche   left
   à gauche   to the left
   sur la gauche   on the left
gendarme *m.*   policeman
gendarmerie *f.*   police station
gendre *m.*   son-in-law
général(e)   general
généreux(-euse)   generous
gens *m.pl.*   people
gentil(le)   kind
gentillesse *f.*   kindness
geste *m.*   gesture
gîte *m.*   holiday cottage or flat
glisser   to slide, slip
globe *m.*   globe
goudronné(e)   tarred, asphalted
grain *m.*   grain
grand(e)   big, tall

grande personne   grown-up
grand-mère *f.*   grandmother
grand-oncle *m.*   great-uncle
grave   serious, grave
gros(se)   fat, large
grossesse *f.*   pregnancy
gym *f.*   gym
gymnase *m.*   gymnasium

H

l'   **habitant** *m.*   inhabitant
   habiter   to live in
   habituellement   normally
le   **halage**   towing
   le chemin de halage   towpath
la   **halle**   hall, covered market
la   **hanche**   hip
la   **hardiesse**   boldness
le   **hasard**   chance
   par hasard   by (any) chance
   haut(e)   high
   un haut lieu   major centre
la   **hauteur**   height
l'   **herbe** *f.*   herb, grass
l'   **heure** *f.*   hour, time
   à tout à l'heure   see you later
   heureusement   fortunately
   heureux(-euse)   happy
   hier   yesterday
l'   **hiver** *m.*   winter
l'   **hommage** *m.*   tribute
l'   **homme** *m.*   man
l'   **hôpital** *m.*   hospital
l'   **hôtel** *m.*   hotel, mansion
   humain(e)   human
   humanitaire   humanitarian
   humide   humid
l'   **hyper-centre** *m.*   very centre

I

ici   here
   d'ici là   between now and then
île *f.*   island
imiter   to imitate
importance *f.*   importance, size
n'importe comment   any old how
n'importe qui   anybody at all
n'importe quoi   anything at all
impôt *m.*   tax
impression *f.*   impression
incendie m.   fire
incompétent(e)   incompetent
inconnu(e)   unknown
indéterminé(e)   undetermined, open-ended
indice *m.*   indication, sign
industrie *f.*   industry
industriel(le)   industrial
inégalité *f.*   inequality
infernal(e)   hellish
information *f.*   information

informatique *f.*   information technology
infrastructure *f.*   infrastructure
ingénieur *m.*   engineer
inoubliable   unforgettable
inquiétant(e)   worrying
inscription *f.*   enrolment
insolence *f.*   insolence
instant *m.*   instant, moment
instrument *m.*   instrument
intention *f.*   intention
   avoir l'intention de   to intend to
interdire   to forbid, ban
intéressant(e)   interesting
intéressé(e)   interested
intérieur(e)   internal *n.m.* interior
intervieweur(-euse)   interviewer
inutile   useless
invitation *f.*   invitation
isoler   to isolate
itinéraire *m.*   itinerary
itinérant(e)   itinerant

J

jamais   ever, never
jambe *f.*   leg
jardin *m.*   garden
jeep *f.*   jeep
jeter   to throw, throw away
jeune   young
jouer   to play
jouet *m.*   toy
jour *m.*   day
   au jour d'aujourd'hui   at this moment in time
journal *m.*   newspaper
journée *f.*   day
juillet *m.*   July
juin *m.*   June
jusqu'à   until, as far as
juste   just
justement   precisely
justice *f.*   justice

K

kilomètre *m.*   kilometre

L

là   there
là-bas   over there
label m.   label
laisser   to leave
langue *f.*   language, tongue
lanterne *f.*   sidelight
larguer   to loose, release
lavage *m.*   wash
lave-vaisselle *m.*   dishwasher
légèrement   lightly
lendemain *m.*   next day
lequel (laquelle)   (the) which

lessive *f.*   washing, washing powder/liquid
lettre *f.*   letter
leur   their
lever   to raise;
   se lever   to get (oneself) up
liberté *f.*   liberty
libre   free
licenciement *m.*   dismissal, redundancy
lieu *m.*   place;
   avoir lieu   to take place
ligne *f.*   line
limite *f.*   limit
   à la limite   you could even say
linge *m.*   clothes, linen
liquide *m.*   liquid
lire   to read
lit *m.*   bed
livre *f.*   pound
livre *m.*   book
local(e)   local; *n.m.* (often *pl.* **locaux**) place, premises
locataire *m.* or *f.*   tenant
location *f.*   hiring, rental
logement *m.*   housing
loger   to live, accommodate
loisirs *m.pl.*   leisure
longtemps   a long time
lorsque   when
lot *m.*   prize, plot
louer   to hire, rent
lourd(e)   heavy
loyer *m.*   rent
lumière *f.*   light
lunaire   lunar
lutter   to struggle
luxuriant(e)   lush
lyrique   lyrical

M

machine *f.*   machine
   machine à laver   washing machine
magasin *m.*   shop
magnétique   magnetic
magnétoscope *m.*   video recorder
magnifique   magnificent
main *f.*   hand
maintenant   now
maintenir   to maintain
maire *m.*   mayor
mairie *f.*   town hall
mais   but
maison *f.*   house, firm
maison-mère *f.*   mother-house
mal   badly
   avoir mal   to have a pain
malade   ill; *n.m.* or *f.* sick person
maladie *f.*   illness
malheureusement   unfortunately
mandater   to mandate
manger   to eat
manière *f.*   manner

manifestation *f.* activity demonstration
manœuvre *f.* manoeuvre
manquer to be lacking
    tu me manques I miss you
manteau *m.* coat
marchandises *f.* goods
marcher to walk; (of machine) to work
mardi *m.* Tuesday
mari *m.* husband
mariage *m.* marriage
marié(e) married
marquer to mark
Mars *m.* Mars
mars *m.* March
martien(ne) Martian
masque *m.* mask
mauvais(e) bad
médecin *m.* doctor
médecine *f.* medicine
médias *m.pl.* media
médical(e) medical
meilleur(e) better
mélange *m.* mixture
mélanger to mix
membre *m.* member, limb
même even, same
mémoire *f.* memory
ménage *m.* household, housework
mendiant(e) beggar
mener to lead
mer *f.* sea
mercredi *m.* Wednesday
mère *f.* mother
mérite *m.* merit
merveilleux(-euse) marvellous
mesure *f.* measure
méthode *f.* method, course
métier *m.* trade, profession
Métropole *f.* metropolitan France
mettre to put
meulière: pierre *f.* **meulière** millstone, buhrstone
meurtre *m.* murder
Midi *m.* the south of France
midi midday, 12 noon
mieux better; **tant mieux!** so much the better!
milieu *m.* middle, milieu
militaire military; *n.m.* soldier
million *m.* million
ministère *m.* ministry
ministre *m.* minister
minuit midnight
mission *f.* mission
mode *f.* fashion; *m.* method
moins less; **au moins** at least
mois *m.* month
moment *m.* moment
mon (ma) mes my
monastère *m.* monastery
monde *m.* world, people
    tout le monde everybody
monnaie *f.* change, currency
montagne *f.* mountain
montagneux(-euse) mountainous

monter to go up
montre *f.* watch
montrer to show
monument *m.* monument
mort(e) dead
mort *f.* death
moulin *m.* mill
    moulin à vent windmill
mourir to die
mouvement *m.* movement
moyen(ne) middle, average
    moyen *m.* means
    moyen âge Middle Ages
    moyenne *f.* statistical mean, pass-mark
muraille *f.* wall
musée *m.* museum
musique *f.* music

N

nager to swim
naître to be born
naturel(le) natural
naturellement naturally
nécessaire necessary
nécessiter to necessitate
négatif, -ive negative
neuf(-ve) new
niveau *m.* level
noces *f.pl.* wedding
nocturne nocturnal
nom *m.* name, surname
nombre *m.* number
nommé(e) named
nord *m.* north
normalement normally
notamment notably
notre, nos our
nourrir to feed
nouveau, nouvel (before vowel), **(nouvelle)** new
    nouvelle(s) *n.f.* news
nuage *m.* cloud
nucléaire nuclear
nuit *f.* night

O

obligatoire obligatory
observation *f.* observation
occasion *f.* opportunity
    d'occasion second-hand
occidental(e) western
occuper to occupy
    s'occuper de to look after
océan *m.* ocean
œuvre *f.* work, charity
office *m.* office, duties, church service, pantry
offrir to give
oiseau *m.* bird
ombragé(e) shaded
ombre *f.* shade

on one, you, we
or *m.* gold
or now
ordinaire ordinary
ordre *m.* order
originaire de originating from, native of
originalité *f.* originality
origine *f.* origin
orteil *m.* toe
ou or; **ou…ou** either…or
où where (also when)
oublier to forget
ouvrir to open

P

paiement *m.* payment
paix *f.* peace
palmier *m.* palm-tree
panne *f.* breakdown (of machine, *esp.* car)
   en panne broken down
   en panne d'essence out of petrol
panneau *m.* panel, notice board, roadsign
papier *m.* paper
paquet *m.* package, parcel
paquet-cadeau *m.* gift-wrapped parcel
par by; **par contre** on the other hand
paralysé(e) paralysed
paralysie *f.* paralysis
parce que because
parebrise *m.* windscreen
parent *m.* parent, relative
parfait(e) perfect
parking *m.* car-park
parler to speak, talk
parmi among
parole *f.* word
part *f.* share, portion
   d'une part on the one hand
partager share
participant *m.* participant
particulier(-ère) private
   hôtel particulier private mansion
particulièrement particularly
partie *f.* part
partiel(le) partial
partir to leave
partout everywhere
pas du tout not at all
passeport *m.* passport
passer to pass, spend (time)
   se passer to happen
pastel *m.* blue dye made from woad
patrimoine *m.* heritage
pauvre poor
payer to pay
pays *m.* country, region
paysage *m.* landscape
pêche *f.* fishing, peach
peinture *f.* painting
pèlerinage *m.* pilgrimage
penchant *m.* tendency, liking

pendant during
péniche *f.* barge
penser to think
perdre to lose
père *m.* father
   le Père Noël Father Christmas
période *f.* period
périple *m.* tour, voyage
permanence *f.* permanence, office, time when
   someone is on duty
permettre to permit, allow
permis *m.* permit, licence
   permis de conduire driving licence
perpétuer to perpetuate
perroquet *m.* parrot
personne *f.* person
   (with **ne** or alone) nobody
personnel(le) personal
personnellement personally
petit(e) small
   petit(e) ami(e) boy(girl)friend
   un petit peu a little
petit-enfant *m.* grandchild
peu little; **un peu** a little
   à peu près approximately
peur *f.* fear; **avoir peur** to be afraid
peut-être perhaps
phare *m.* headlight
pharmacie *f.* pharmacy, chemist's
photo *f.* photo
piano *m.* piano
pièce *f.* room, piece, part, coin
pied *m.* foot
   pied-noir *m.* French person born in Algeria
pierre *f.* stone
piéton *m.* pedestrian
pile *f.* stack, battery, tails (of coin)
piqueniquer to picnic
pire *adj.* worse
   de pire en pire worse and worse
pis *adv.* worse; **tant pis!** too bad!
piscine *f.* swimming pool
piste *f.* track
   piste cyclable cycle track
pittoresque picturesque
place *f.* space, square, seat
plage *f.* beach
plaie *f.* wound
de plaisance pleasure (cruising)
plaisir *m.* pleasure
planétaire planetary
planète *f.* planet
planning *m.* schedule
planter to plant
plaque *f.* sheet, slab, plate, hotplate
plâtre *m.* plaster
plein(e) full
   plein de lots of, plenty of
pleuvoir (il pleut) to rain
plomb *m.* lead
   sans plomb unleaded
plongée *f.* diving
plus more; **le (la) plus** the most

plus ou moins   more or less
plusieurs   several
plutôt   rather
pneu *m.*   tyre
poésie *f.*   poetry
poignet *m.*   wrist
point *m.*   point; **point de vue** viewpoint
   point mort   neutral (gear)
poisson *m.*   fish
politique   political; *n.f.* politics
population *f.*   population
porte *f.*   door
porter   to carry, wear
portefeuille *m.*   wallet
Portugal *m.*   Portugal
positif(-ive)   positive
posséder   to possess
possibilité *f.*   possibility
pot *m.*   pot, glass, drink, luck
poubelle *f.*   dustbin
poule *f.*   hen
pourquoi   why
pousser   to push
pouvoir   to be able
pratique   practical
pratiquement   practically
précis(e)   precise
précisément   precisely
préciser   to specify
préférer   to prefer
préjudice *m.*   loss, damage, wrong
prélavage *m.*   prewash
premier(-ère)   first
premièrement   first of all
prenant(e)   absorbing, fascinating
prendre   to take
près   near; **à peu près** approximately
   près de   near to
   tout près   very near
présence *f.*   presence
présenter   to present, introduce
préserver   to preserve
presque   nearly
prestige *m.*   prestige
prêt(e)   ready
prétexte *m.* pretext
prévoir   to plan, foresee
prier   to implore
   je vous en prie I beg you / don't mention it
primordial(e)   essential
prise *f.* **de son**   sound recording
privé(e)   private
privilège *m.*   privilege
problème *m.*   problem
prochain(e)   next
produit *m.*   product, chemical
professionnel(le)   professional
profil *m.*   profile
profond(e)   profound, deep
profondément   profoundly, deeply
programme *m.*   programme
projet *m.*   project, plan
se promener   to go for a walk

promouvoir   to promote
proposition *f.*   offer, suggestion
propre   clean, own
propriétaire *m.* or *f.*   owner
protection *f.*   protection
protéger   to protect
Provence *f.*   Provence
province *f.*   province
   en province   in the provinces
publier   to publish
puce *f.*   flea, micro-chip
   ma puce   term of endearment
puis   then
puisque   since
puissance *f.*   power
pull *m.*   pullover, sweater

Q

qu'est-ce que?   what? (object)
qu'est-ce qui?   what? (subject)
qualité *f.*   quality
quand   when
quand même   really, still, all the same
quant à   as for
quantité *f.*   quantity
quartier *m.*   district
que   whom, which; **que?** what?
quel(le)   which
quelqu'un   someone
quelque chose   something
quelques   a few
question *f.*   question
qui   who, which; **qui?** who? whom?
quoi   what

R

radio *f.*   radio, X-ray
raison *f.*   reason; **avoir raison** to be right
râler   to moan
ramener   to bring back
ranger   to put away
rapatrier   to repatriate
rapide   rapid
rappeler   to remind
   se rappeler   to remember
rassurer   to assure, reassure
ravi(e)   delighted
ravissant(e)   delightful
réaction *f.*   reaction
réalisation *f.*   creation, production,
   achievement, carrying out
réaliser   to realise, carry out, fulfil
réalité *f.*   reality
récent(e)   recent
récepteur *m.*   receiver
recevoir   to receive
rechange: pneu de rechange   spare tyre
recharger   to recharge
réchauffer   to heat up (again)

rechercher to seek
récif *m.* reef
récolte *f.* harvest
récolter to harvest, collect
récompenser to recompense
réconforter to comfort
reçu *m.* receipt
recueillir to gather
récupérer to obtain, recover, collect
redonner to give again, give back
réduire to reduce
réellement really
réfectoire *m.* refectory
réfléchir to reflect, to think
réforme *f.* reform
refuser to refuse
regard *m.* look
regarder to look at
région *f.* region
régional(e) regional
règles *f.pl.* (menstrual) period
régulièrement regularly
réintégrer to reintegrate
relâcher to let go
relancer to jump-start
relativement relatively
relier to link, bind
religieux(-euse) religious
remarquable remarkable
remarquer to notice
remercier to thank
remettre to put back, put off
remporter to carry off
remuer to stir
renaissance *f.* renaissance, rebirth
rencontre *f.* encounter
rencontrer to meet
rendement *m.* (financial) return
rendez-vous *m.* appointment
renseignement *m.* piece of information
rentrée *f.* return to school/university
rentrer to go in, go home
réparable repairable
répartir to share out
repas *m.* meal
repassage *m.* ironing
répondre to answer
représenter to represent
réputé(e) famous
requin *m.* shark
réserve *f.* reserve, stock
réserver to reserve, book
résidence *f.* residence, block of flats
résidentiel(le) residential
respecter to respect
reste *m.* remainder
rester to stay
retard *m.* delay, lateness
retenir to retain, detain
retomber to fall down again
retour *m.* return
retourner to return
retransmettre to retransmit

retrouver to find
réunir to bring together
  se réunir to meet, get together
réussir to succeed
rêve *m.* dream
révéler to reveal
revenir to come back
revoir to see again; **au revoir!** goodbye!
riche rich
richesse *f.* richness
ridicule ridiculous
rien (often with **ne**) nothing
rive *f.* bank
rocher *m.* rock
rôle *m.* role
roman(e) Romanesque
roman *m.* novel
rose pink; *n.f.* rose
rouge red
rouler to roll, drive
route *f.* road
rue *f.* street
ruée *f.* rush
rythme *m.* rhythm

S

sable *m.* sand
sacoche *m.* bag
safari *m.* safari
saigner to bleed
Saint-Valentin *f.* Valentine's day
saisonnier(-ère) seasonal
salle *f.* **de bains** bathroom
salon *m.* drawing/living room
samedi *m.* Saturday
sang-froid *m.* composure
sans without
sans-abri *m.* or *f.* homeless person
satellite *m.* satellite
satirique satirical
satisfaire to satisfy
sauf except for
saumon *m.* salmon
sauter to jump, blow
sauvage wild
sauvegarder to protect
savoir to know, be able to
scandalisé(e) scandalised, shocked
scientifique scientific
sculpture *f.* sculpture
séance *f.* session, showing
secondaire secondary
secourir to help, aid, rescue
secours *m.* help, aid; **au secours!** help!
séjour *m.* stay
séjourner to stay
semaine *f.* week
sembler to seem
sens *m.* sense, direction; **dans le mauvais sens** the wrong way round
sentiment *m.* feeling

---

septembre *m.*   September
serpent *m.* **de mer**   sea serpent
service *m.*   service; **services sociaux**   social services
servir   to serve
session *f.*   session, sitting
seul(e)   sole, alone
seulement   only
sévère   severe
sexe *m.*   sex
siècle *m.*   century
silence *m.*   silence
simple   simple, single
simplicité *f.*   simplicity
singe *m.*   monkey
site *m.*   site
situation *f.*   situation
situé(e)   situated
ski *m.*   ski, skiing
skier   to ski
social(e)   social
société *f.*   society
sœur *f.*   sister
soigner   to look after, tend
soir *m.*   evening
soirée *f.*   evening, party
sol *m.*   ground
solaire   solar
soleil *m.*   sun
solution *f.*   solution, explanation
somptueux(-euse)   sumptuous
sonde *f.*   probe
sorte *f.*   sort
sortir   to go out
souffle *m.*   breath
souffler   to breathe, blow
souffrir   to suffer
souhaiter   to wish for
soûl (pronounced **sou**) **(soûle)**   drunk
sourire   to smile; *n.m.* smile
sous   under
sous-sol *m.*   subsoil, basement
souvenir *m.*   memory, reminder
souvent   often
spécial(e)   special
spécifique   specific
spécimen *m.*   specimen
spectacle *m.*   show
sport *m.*   sport
sportif(-ive)   *adj.* sports, sporty
standardiste *m.* or *f.*   switchboard operator
station de radio *f.*   radio station
station-service *f.*   petrol station
stationnement *m.*   parking
statue *f.*   statue
statuer   to give a ruling
studio *m.*   studio, bed-sit
style *m.*   style
succès *m.*   success
sucré(e)   sweet
sucre *m.*   sugar
sud *m.*   south
suffire   to suffice, be enough

suisse   Swiss
suite à   following
suivre   to follow
sujet *m.*   subject
super   four-star/super petrol
supplémentaire   supplementary
sûr(e)   sure; **bien sûr** of course
surface *f.*   surface
surmonter   to surmount, crown
surtout   above all
survivant(e)   surviving, survivor
susceptible   liable
suspendre   to suspend
symbole *m.*   symbol
sympathique   nice, likeable
syndicat *m.* **d'initiative**   tourist office
système *m.*   system

T

ta *f.* of **ton**
tabac *m.*   tobacco, tobacconist's
tableau *m.*   picture, table
talent *m.*   talent
tambour *m.*   drum
tard   late
tarif *m.*   tariff
tarifaire *adj.*   pricing
taxi *m.*   taxi
technicien(ne)   technician
technique *f.*   technique, applied science
tel (telle)   such, such a
téléphoner   to telephone
télévision *f.*   television
tellement   so, so much
témoin *m.*   witness
temps *m.*   time, weather
    l'emploi du temps   timetable
    de temps en temps   from time to time
tenir   to hold
tennis *m.*   tennis, game of tennis
tenter   to tempt, attempt
terminer   to finish, complete
terre *f.*   earth
territoire *m.*   territory
tête *f.*   head
théâtre *m.*   theatre
toi-même   yourself
toilettes *f.pl.*   toilet
toit *m.*   roof
tomber   to fall
ton (ta) tes   your
top *m.*   top of the charts
tort *m.*   wrong; **avoir tort** to be wrong
tortue *f.*   tortoise
total(e)   total
toucan *m.*   toucan
toujours   always, still
toulousain(e)   from Toulouse
tour *f.*   tower; *m.* circumference
    tour *m.* **du monde**   world tour
tourisme *m.*   tourism

touristique touristic, touristy
tourmenter to torment
tourner to turn
tout (toute), tous (toutes) all
    tout à fait absolutely
    tout à l'heure! see you later!
    tout d'abord first of all
    tout de suite immediately
    tout le monde everybody
train *m.* train; **en train de** in the process of
traitement *m.* treatment, processing
transformer to transform
transmettre to convey, transmit
transparent(e) transparent
transport *m.* transport
transporter to transport
travail *m.* work
travailler to work
trier to sort
tronc *m.* trunk, collecting box
trop too, too much
trophée *m.* trophy
tropical(e) tropical
trouver to find; **se trouver** to be situated
truquage *m.* special effects
tuba *m.* snorkel
tuer to kill
tulipe *f.* tulip
tunisien(ne) Tunisian
tuyau *m.* pipe, tip

U

uni(e) united
unique unique, only
uniquement only
unité *f.* unity
utilisateur *m.* user
utiliser to use
utopique utopian

V

vacances *f.pl.* holiday
vaisselle *f.* crockery, washing-up
valable valid
varier to vary
vaste vast
végétal(e) *adj.* plant
végétation *f.* vegetation
véhicule *m.* vehicle
vélo *m.* bicycle
vendre to sell
venir to come
vent *m.* wind
verdict *m.* verdict

véritable veritable, real
verre *m.* glass
vers towards
verser to pour
vêtement *m.* garment
vétérinaire veterinary
viande *f.* meat
vie *f.* life, living
vieux, vieil (before vowel) **(vieille)** old
vigueur *f.* strength
    entrer en vigueur to come into effect
village *m.* village
ville *f.* town
vin *m.* wine
vingtaine *f.* about twenty
vingtième twentieth
violence *f.* violence
visiter to visit
vite fast
vitesse *f.* speed, gear
vitre *f.* window pane
vivre to live
vocation *f.* vocation, calling
voici here (it) is, here (they) are
voie *f.* track
voilà there (it) is, there (they) are
voir to see
voisin(e) neighbour
voiture *f.* car
voix *f.* voice
vol *m.* flight, theft
volcan *m.* volcano
voler to fly, steal
voleur *m.* thief
volontiers willingly
voter to vote
votre, vos your
vouloir to want
    vouloir dire to mean
vous-même yourself
voyage *m.* journey
voyager to travel
vrai(e) real, true
vraiment really, truly
vue *f.* sight, view

W

week-end *m.* weekend

Y

y there, to it
yeux *m.pl. (sing.* **œil***)* eyes

GRAMMAR CONTENTS
AND CONVERSATIONS

A unit-by-unit guide to the grammar taught in the course and the titles of the Conversations

---

GRAMMAR INDEX

Page-references to explanations of grammar points

Have you enjoyed this course? Want to learn more?

Breakthrough Languages

Ideal for self-study . Practise and develop your skills . Learn a new language

Level 1 beginner's courses

Easy-to-use book and cassette or CD* courses.

Availablein French, Spanish, German, Italian, Greek and Chinese.

* CDs for French and Spanish only.

Also available online for French and Spanish Level 1:

For students:

Multi-choice grammar exercises

For teachers:

Photocopiable exercise sheets, teacher's notes and tapescripts

For all courses:

A free site licence is available on request permitting duplication of audio material for

Taking it further

Level 2 in Spanish, French and German
Level 3 in French

Increase your vocabulary, fluency and confidence with these higher level book and cassette courses.

Available from all good bookshops, or direct from Palgrave Macmillan.
Please call Macmillan Direct on 01256 302866
All course books are available on inspection to teaching staff where an adoption would result in the sale of 12 or more copies. Please email lecturerservices@palgrave.com
For further information log on to
www.palgrave.com/breakthrough

Extra practice

Activity Books with imaginative and varied exercises

Available for Level 1 French, Spanish and German

www.palgrave.com/breakthrough